Media Ethics and Regulation:
Insights from Africa

I0094512

Editor
Christina Chan-Meetoo

Langaa Research & Publishing CIG
Mankon, Bamenda

Publisher
Langaa RPCIG
Langaa Research & Publishing Common Initiative Group
P.O. Box 902 Mankon
Bamenda
North West Region
Cameroon
Langaagrp@gmail.com
www.langaa-rpcig.net

Distributed in and outside N. America by African Books Collective
orders@africanbookscollective.com
www.africanbookcollective.com

ISBN: 9956-790-11-7

Foreword

It goes without saying that media, nowadays, has a strong impact on our lives. It democratizes access to information in all fields. It contributes to shape societies.

Our modern world has witnessed a higher degree of interconnectivity. We are basically a global village where the flow of information enables news to travel more easily across technological, social, and geographical boundaries. All in a matter of seconds.

As an educator and shaper of public opinion, media has a pivotal role. It is therefore of paramount importance that media people be aware of the impact of their reports on not only the actors of their articles but also on the general public. In this perspective, journalists and editors should promote responsible reporting in a bid to mitigate gender discrimination and push for positive change.

This Gender Code of Ethics for the Media highlights the importance of upholding high standards of ethics. It can facilitate the elimination of existing discriminative practices in media and contribute to the production of more gender sensitive content.

A critical look at the Mauritian context has served as basis for the elaboration of this book. It can be used by an individual, but can also prove useful to local media houses in the pursuit of more professional reporting.

Indeed, abiding by a set of principles of ethics and fairness as well as acknowledging responsibility for one's story, ensures that offences are mitigated. It also allows for the respect of the integrity of parties concerned.

As women become more and more the object of interest of media professionals, the adoption of a gender code of ethics takes increasing relevancy.

Indeed, the adoption of strong ethical reporting demarcates sensationalism of news from true journalism. If those values are adopted across the board, the press will have accomplished its primary aim: that of being free to inform but in a responsible way in our democratic society.

Hon Mrs Mireille Martin
Minister of Gender Equality, Child Development and Family Welfare
Republic of Mauritius
July 2013

Contents

Foreword

With the difficult economic conditions for media houses, the emergence of new technologies which give rise to citizen journalism, the fierce competition for attention in a hyper-mediated environment, journalism seems to be in constant turmoil. The temptation to have recourse to paycheck journalism, sensationalist news coverage and mere trivia to seduce an elusive audience is strong. Yet the very lowering of standards can only further undermine the credibility of a noble profession which purports to act as a watchdog, a Fourth Estate in a democratic society.

In a world full of moral contradictions and dilemmas, journalism must show that it has the right moral compass to live up to its claims of being an intellectual force which can enlighten the masses. Political and economic decision-makers are expected to bow to demands for transparency and accountability. Similarly, media houses and journalists need to show that they live up to their social contract with their readers, listeners and viewers. Claims that ethics is a private affair no longer hold good and mechanisms for monitoring and promoting ethical practice in journalism are essential.

This book thus aims to help journalists navigate the difficult issues which they continuously face in the exercise of their profession. In the first chapter, Francis Nyamnjoh redefines the contours of professional ethics in journalism within the context of our cultural belonging to Africanity. The second chapter, written by Christina Chan-Meetoo provides a useful insight into the minds of Mauritian

1

journalists who assess their own industry and makes a case for industry self-regulation. In the next three chapters, Johan Retief proposes an in-depth examination of the South African model of independent co-regulation. The sixth chapter, written by Bruno Albin, charts out the difficulties of ethical regulation in France. In the last two chapters, the authors, Sheila Bunwaree and Christina Chan-Meetoo, stress on the importance of a gender approach to ethics as it is felt that the media have a moral duty to significantly mitigate the effects of gender discrimination both within their content and their own internal structures. A Gender Code of Ethics for the Media is also proposed for adoption by media houses and journalists.

To a large extent, this publication is inspired by the two workshops which were conducted in Mauritius in October 2012. These workshops and this book would not have been possible were it not for the support of the UNESCO agency IPDC (International Programme for the Development of Communication) and of the University of Mauritius. Our sincere gratitude goes to both institutions.

Our sincere thanks go to Al-Amin Yusuph from the Dar-es-Salaam office for supporting the initiative. Many thanks to Deepa Gokulsing for her tremendous help in organising the workshops, to Ramola Ramtohul for her useful assistance and to Gender Links for their input in the Gender-Sensitive Reporting workshop.

Many thanks also to Francis Nyamnjoh for agreeing to contribute one chapter to this new edition.

ABOUT THE AUTHORS

Francis B. Nyamnjoh is Professor of Anthropology at the University of Cape Town in South Africa

Christina Chan-Meetoo is Lecturer in Media and Communication at the University of Mauritius.

Johan Retief is Ombudsman for the Press Council of South Africa.

Bruno Albin is a former senior journalist at France Télévisions and France Inter.

Sheila Bunwaree is Professor of Development and Gender Studies at the University of Mauritius.

AFRICA'S MEDIA: BETWEEN PROFESSIONAL ETHICS AND CULTURAL BELONGING

Francis B.Nyamnjoh

1. On the Politics of Belonging in Africa

In 2005 I published *Africa's Media: Democracy and the Politics of Belonging*. One of the main findings of that study was that the media have assumed a partisan, highly politicised, militant role in Africa. They have done so by dividing citizens into the righteous and the wicked, depending on their party-political leanings, ideologies, regional, cultural or ethnic belonging. By considering the Cameroonian experience, the book sought to understand how scapegoatism, partisanship, and regional and ethnic tendencies in the media have affected their liberal democratic responsibility to act as honest, fair and neutral mediators – accessible to all and sundry. It did this by looking at polarisation in the press and at how the media have shaped and been shaped by the politics of belonging since the early 1990s.

Almost everywhere in Cameroon, citizens expect the urban elite – including journalists and media proprietors – to make inroads into the modern centres of accumulation. Since the state is a major source of patronage and resources, it, together with other economic institutions, must be manipulated to divert the flow of finance, jobs and so forth to the home regions from which

5

the heterogeneous urban originally derive. Thus these elites are under pressure to act as facilitators and manipulators with respect to the state. Through elite development associations, they lobby foreign agencies and NGOs to provide their home villages or regions with new sources of wealth and livelihood. In return for so doing, they may be rewarded with neo-traditional titles in their home villages. These honours confer on them symbolic capital that is not expressed in material wealth but sustained by what Fisiy and Goheen have termed 'the conspicuous display of decorum and accompanied by public respect' (1998:388), that in turn can always be exploited for political ends at regional and national levels. In certain cases, investing in the village is a way of consolidating success in the city, especially in the politics of ethno-regionalism.

As many scholars of Cameroon have observed, these modern big men and women who live with one foot in the city and the other in the village, are able to redistribute their personal wealth to those back in the home village in exchange for neo-traditional titles, while continuing to take advantage of the economic and political opportunities made available by the city. In this way, they continue to take an active role in the cultural affairs, government and development of their home areas. At the same time their rural ties lead them to consider customary law and local opinion when making national decisions. They thus become, in the words of mitzi Goheen, 'mediators between the local and national arenas, the interpreters as well as the architects of the intersections between customary and national law.' This is a project for which the elite concerned recruit journalists and the media for purposes of information, communication and public relations within and between communities, and also with the state and the outside world. In Cameroon, almost every appointment and promotion into high office is the prerogative of the President, and most appointed ministers and director general of state corporations have the tendency of returning to their home villages to celebrate and express gratitude to the President with kin and kith. This would seem to suggest that they are appointed primarily to take care of the interests of their home villages or regions at the centre of power, and are only marginally at the service of all and sundry.

In the light of this reality of primary patriotism to the home village by the power elite, the book points to a tension between dominant normative theories of journalism that demand of journalists professional independence and detachment, and the conflicting loyalties to cultural and ethnic communities. The result is a situation where:

> African world-views and cultural values are hence doubly excluded: first by the ideology of hierarchies of cultures, and second by cultural industries more interested in profits than the promotion of creative diversity and cultural plurality. The consequence is an idea of democracy hardly informed by popular articulations of personhood and agency in Africa, and media whose professional values are not in tune with the expectations of those they purport to serve. The predicament of media practitioners in such a situation is obvious: to be of real service to liberal democracy, they must ignore alternative ideas of personhood and agency in the cultural communities of which they are part. Similarly, attending to the interests of particular cultural groups risks contradicting the principles of liberal democracy and its emphasis on the autonomous individual. Torn between such competing and conflicting understandings of democracy, the media find it increasingly difficult to marry rhetoric with practice, and for strategic instrumentalist reasons may opt for a Jekyll and hyde personality. (2005:2-3)

The Cameroonian case study points to the interconnectedness and interpenetration that one might expect between citizenship and subjection, the cosmopolitan and the local, the individual and the collective, that make popular understandings of democracy

7

in Africa far more complex than simplistic notions of liberal democracy would otherwise suggest.

While the book clearly highlights the shortcomings of ethnicised and politicised media in liberal democratic terms, it also points to the limitations of liberal democracy in a context where people are obliged or ready and willing to be both citizens and subjects. They identify with their ethnic group or cultural community on the one hand (ethnic or cultural citizenship), and the nation-state on the other (civic citizenship). The argument for democracy both as an individual and a community or cultural right cannot simply be dismissed when there are individuals who, for one reason or another, straddle both the realm of individual rights (liberal democracy) and the realm of group rights.

As the book maintains, a major characteristic of Africa's second liberation struggles since the 1980s has been a growing obsession with belonging and the questioning of traditional assumptions about nationality and citizenship almost everywhere. Identity politics are central to the political process. Exclusionary conceptions of nationality and citizenship have increased. Group claims for greater cultural recognition are countered by efforts to maintain the status quo of an inherited colonial hierarchy of ethnic groupings. As ethnic groups, either local majorities or minorities, clamour for status they are countered by an often aggressive reaffirmation of age-old exclusions informed by colonial registers of inequalities amongst the subjected. This development is paralleled by an increased distinction between 'locals' and 'foreigners' and between 'indigens' and 'settlers' within and between countries, with the emphasis on opportunities and economic entitlements.

Even in South Africa and Botswana where the economy is relatively better off than elsewhere in sub-Saharan Africa, xenophobia is rife against migrants from other African countries with economic downturns. Referred to derogatorily as 'makwerekwere' (meaning those incapable of articulating local languages that epitomise economic success and power), some of these migrants come from countries that were very instrumental in the struggle against apartheid. Such tensions and boundaries between 'undeserving outsiders' and 'entitled nationals', are eloquently captured by the late Phaswane mpe in Welcome to Our hillbrow, a novel about a part of Johannesburg where 'citizens' fear to tread because criminal and violent makwerekwere have welcomed themselves to and imposed a reign of terror (mphe 2001).

Even South African nationals from the ghettoes, townships and bantustans of the former apartheid dispensation, who are yet to graduate from subjection into citizenship in real terms, have been co-opted by the rhetoric of abundance and success under threat from unregulated immigration. Polarisations and tensions are exacerbated by the racialised lexicon, categorisation and registers of the apartheid era that have fed into the new South Africa, where even progressive academics and media are in no hurry to deconstruct and reconstruct. A consequence, by no means the only, is that South Africans of Indian descent came under a scathing attack in a pop tune by mbongeni Ngema, a popular zulu musician. Titled Ama-Ndiya, the controversial song claims to 'begin a constructive discussion that would lead to a true reconciliation between Indians and Africans', and accuses South African Indians of opportunism and of enriching themselves to the detriment of Blacks, who are presented as more indigenous but most exploited nationals. If the Indians are to be taken seriously as belonging to South Africa, they must display greater patriotism and stop straddling continents. In this way, elite capitalism becomes less of the problem, as black nationals for whom socio- economic citizenship remains an illusion scapegoat makwerekwere and increasingly Asians. This raises questions about the meaning of the juridico-political citizenship guaranteed by the constitution (often touted as the most liberal in the world) of the new South Africa where the socio-economic and cultural cleavages of the apartheid era are yet to be undone in a way that is beneficial to the majority of the victims of apartheid.

Everywhere in Africa, traditional policies of inclusion and emphasis on wealth-in-people over wealth-in-things are under pressure from the politics of entitlements in an era of accelerated flows of capital and migrants, and a context where governments of weak states feel obliged to be repressive while keeping up appearances of democracy. The book argues that in discussions of the media, democracy and rights, this heightened sense of cultural identity cannot simply be dismissed as 'tribalism' and consigned to the past. Again, the Cameroonian experience offers interesting empirical material to inform discussions of how to marry liberal democracy with African cultural, historical, indigenous political and economic realities.

2. Reconciling Professionalism and Cultural Belonging in African Journalism

In view of these tension and conflict between professionalism and cultural belonging in African journalism, I would like, in this lecture, to critically examine conventional journalism in Africa, discuss its shortcomings, and point to the creative processes underway in the lives of ordinary Africans as the way forward for meaningful journalism on the continent and on Africa. The lecture also explores the role of innovations in Information and Communication Technologies (ICTs) in mitigating victimhood and promoting more democratic journalism from the standpoint of how ordinary Africans appropriate the ICTs as individuals and communities. my experience with journalism in Africa and Africa in journalism (JAAJ) is primarily as a consumer of journalistic production and also as an observer of journalists and journalism at work. As a little boy crumpled newspapers were always the bearers of good news, as I would watch in anticipation as my mother unwrapped them to reveal their contents of akara beans, puff balls, bread, groundnuts or whatever other consumer goodies she had bought from the market woman, shopkeeper or street vendor. Then unsold newspapers were simply worth their weight in gold, even though I couldn't quite read them, unless of course they contained interesting pictures.

I grew up appreciating newspapers in other ways too. I remember making clips of newspapers that had brought me good news, such as when they published the results of the various examinations in which I had succeeded, including, in 1986 when I obtained a Cameroonian government scholarship to pursue a doctoral degree in media and communication studies. I proceeded to the Centre for mass Communication Research at the University of leicester, where consuming JAAJ became a scholarly compulsion, and observing journalists a professional impulse, graduating with a PhD, which some would insist stands for: 'Permanent head Damage' or 'Phenomenal Dumbness'. Back unemployed in Cameroon in the early 1990s when the winds of democratization were rustling the baobabs of dictatorship, I was able to sustain my appetite for the multiplicity of newspapers that proliferated the newsstands with colourful and screaming headlines, only thanks to the fact I could pick them up a few days later at almost no cost from market women and storekeepers who were used to buying the unsold in devalued bulk, determined to put them to better use.

As for the broadcast media, I grew up listening to national radio on shortwave band, which was as liberating as it was dictatorial, as I recall how state functionaries used to be hired and fired, promoted and demoted mainly through the radio, which faithfully and regularly broadcast the thunderous outbursts of 'The Great Dictator' or his dogs of war against freedoms. Civil Servants would breakfast, lunch and dine glued to their radio in a mixture of expectation, uncertainty and foreboding, as radio could make them eat with joyous relish, just as it could make them lose their appetite, throw up or faint. Television, which came much later in the mid 1980s to crown the reign of 'Face Powder Democracy' with coloured vision, simply enshrined the dictatorship of the radio, as functionaries have failed to know any better in real terms.

Not to mention the masses swimming at the margins of freedom and opportunity.

Behind every newspaper, radio or television, behind every journalism, African or otherwise, is The Journalist as a socially produced being desperately seeking professionalism in a context of often competing and conflicting demands on their talents and calling. Often, I have wished I were a journalist, but when I watch African journalists at work, when I scrutinize the challenges facing them daily and fathom the compromises they have to make, I thank God I am only a journalist to be.

African Journalism is like swimming upstream most of the time, given all the hurdles journalists and the media face in our various countries. A lot of media freedom advocacy groups, journalists and media scholars, myself included, have catalogued the daily economic, political, institutional and professional constraints confronting African journalists. Amongst these are the tendency by African governments towards excessive centralization, bureaucratization and politicization of state owned media institutions, making it very difficult for state-employed journalists to reconcile the government's expectations with their professional beliefs, or with the expectations of the public. Also stifling, especially for the critical non-government media and journalists, are the legal frameworks regulating the press in many an African country. The craving by most states to control leaves little doubt about how the lawmakers see journalists as potential troublemakers who must be policed. In some countries, even when certain draconian aspects of the press laws of the one-party era have been replaced with new provisions that are relatively more tolerant of opposition views and of criticisms, often the selective application of the laws, together with the use of extra-legal measures, have been to the detriment of the critical private press, and have made it very difficult for this press to have the professional independence its needs. Other factors adversely affecting African Journalism include widespread job insecurity, poor salaries and poor working conditions of most journalists. Financial difficulties, lack of personnel and inadequate specialization or professionalization, ignorance of the market, and the uncertainties of life in the age of flexible mobility and its paradoxes, have only compounded the predicaments of African Journalism. Even when NGOs and other organizations intervene to assist the media financially and otherwise, they often resort to abstract and rigid notions of freedom that make them appear more like religious fundamentalists – what harri Englund as termed 'human Rights Fundamentalists' in his study of rights activitists in malawi and their deafness to alternative perspectives and the lived experiences of those they seek to convert.

These, however, are not the challenges that concern me in this lecture. Of concern here are the basic assumptions that underpin African journalism in definition and practice, and the consequences on journalists as socially and politically shaped beings who are part and parcel of the cultural communities in which they pursue their profession. To what extent does journalism as defined and practiced in Africa, adapted to the lived realities and ideas of personhood of the various individuals and communities that claim Africanity?

3. What Is Africanity?

What does it mean to be African? Who qualifies to claim Africa? Is being African or claiming Africa an attribute of race and skin colour (black, white, yellow), birth (umbilical cord, birth certificates, identity cards, passports), geography (physical spaces, home village), history (encounters), culture (prescriptive specificities), economics (availability and affordability, wealth and deprivation), sociology (social configurations and action, inclusion and exclusion), psychology (mind sets), philosophy (world views), politics (power relations), collective memory (shared experiences and aspirations), or a category through which a world that is not rigidly geographical, racial or cultural is constructed, to name just a few of the many possibilities that present themselves? These are questions which have deep roots in debates on citizenship and identity – and, therefore, in the definition of rights, entitlement, duties, and responsibilities. The questions are, of course, not uniquely African - indeed, similar issues have been posed and debated with considerable passion in other parts of the world both historically and currently, and contestations around them have also often been played out in violent communal confrontations, civil wars, and inter-state conflicts. And while they may seem straight forward to answer, the questions have been rendered much more complex by the dynamic inter-play of race, ethnicity, gender and religion in the structuring and exercise of power and opportunity. Precisely for this reason, they are not questions that can be addressed in the abstract.

how one answers the questions that are generated by any attempt at grappling with Africanity is not only situationally determined, but is also a function of how selective one is with regard to the various indicators available. Some individuals and communities on the continent and elsewhere might claim Africanity or have it imposed upon them for various personal, collective, historical and political reasons. But it is not always straight forward to say which of these claims may be legitimate and why, especially as identity is not only how one sees oneself, but also how one is seen and categorised by others, particularly where the absorption of new populations is involved. This is all the more so as identities are themselves always in mutation, shaped as they are by changing historical contexts and circumstances, such as internal and international migrations, shifts in social power relations.

It is, however, safe to say that to most ordinary people in Africa, Africanity is more than just a birth certificate, an identity card, or a passport – documents that many of them may not have, even as others coming from elsewhere and waving the flag of Africanity may have all of these documents and more. For the ordinary person, to be African is not simply to be labelled or merely defined as such. It is to be a social actor/actress enmeshed in a particular context that has been and continues to be shaped by a unique

14

history that, among others, is marked by unequal encounters and misrepresentations often informed by the arrogance and ignorance of the economically and politically powerful who take the liberty also to arrogate a cultural superiority to themselves. For the masses of Africans, Africa is above all a lived reality, one that is constantly shaped and reshaped (socially produced) by their toil and sweat as subjected and devalued humanity, even as they struggle to live in dignity and to transform their societies progressively. For these people, the fact of their Africanity is neither in question nor a question. And the least they would expect from concerned journalists is to refrain from adding onto their burdens in the name of a type of journalism which, in being ahistorical, also trivialises their collective experiences and memories in the guise of a socially and culturally disembedded professional ethic.

4. Problematic Assumptions in African Journalism

The basic assumptions underpinning African Journalism in definition and practice, are not informed by the fact that ordinary Africans are busy Africanizing their modernity and modernizing their Africanity in ways often too complex for simplistic dichotomies to capture. The precepts of journalism that apply currently in Africa are largely at variance with dominant ideas of personhood and agency (and by extension society, culture and democracy) shared by communities across the continent, as it assumes that there is a One-Best-Way of being and doing to which Africans must aspire and be converted in the name of modernity and civilization

– and this, despite the fact that the very modernity and civilization which they are called upon to embrace actively produces and reproduces them as 'different','inferior', and belonging to the'margins' of the forces shaping global processes.

This divorce is at the heart of some of the professional and ethical dilemmas that haunt journalism in and on Africa, a journalism whose tendency is to debase and caricature African humanity,

15

creativity and realities. It is a constraint that renders African Journalism a journalism of bandwagonism, where mimicry is the order of the day, as emphases is less on thinking than on doing, less on leading than on being led, less on defining than on being defined. African Journalism lacks both the power of self-definition and the power to shape the universals that are deaf-and-dumb to the particularities of journalism in and on Africa. Because journalism has tended to be treated as an attribute of so-called 'modern' societies or of 'superior' others, it is only proper, so the reasoning goes, that African Journalism and the societies it serves, are taught the principles and professional practices by those who 'know' what it means to be civilized and to be relevant to civilization in a global hierarchy of humanity and cultures.

Aspiring journalists in Africa must, like containers, be dewatered of the mud and dirt of culture as tradition and custom, and filled afresh with the tested sparkles of culture as modernity and civilization. African journalists are thus called upon to operate in a world where everything has been predefined for them by others, where they are meant to implement and hardly ever to think or rethink, where what is expected of them is respect for canons, not to question how or why canons are forged, or the extent to which canons are inclusive of the creative diversity of the universe that is purportedly of interest to the journalism of the One-Best-Way. And that is not all, since they are defined a priori as inferior and marginal to the forces that shape global journalism, their best journalism is at best second-rate even when they are competing with second-rate others.

5. Humanity, Creativity

how well journalism is relevant to Africa and Africans depends on what value such journalism gives African humanity and creativity. If a journalism is such that privileges a hierarchy of humanity and human creativity, and if such journalism believes that African humanity and creativity are at the abyss of that interconnected global hierarchy, such journalism is bound to be prescriptive, condescending, contrived, caricatured and hardly in tune with the quest by Africans for equality of humanity and for recognition and representation. And if African journalists were to, wittingly or unwittingly, buy into that hierarchy, they would in effect be working against the interests of the very African communities they claim to serve with their journalism. But if one convinces one's self that one is at the abyss, that one is a veritable heart of darkness, one doesn't need much convincing buying into prescriptions on how to fish one's self out of the abyss or the heart of darkness, especially if such prescriptions are by those one has been schooled to recognize and represent as superior, and especially if the latter are in a position of power – if they have the yam and the knife, as Chinua Achebe would put it.

A closer look at democracy in Africa is a good indicator of how journalism has tended to articulate and appreciate African realities through the prescriptive lenses of those who believe their ideas of humanity and creativity to be sufficiently rich and practiced for uncritical adoption by 'emerging' others. In Europe and North America, liberal democracy is said to guarantee journalism the best environment it needs to foster freedom and progress. Liberal democracy's colossal investments in the making of the 'Independent Individual' is projected as the model to be promoted and defended by journalism in and on Africa. yet the more African Journalism strives to implant liberal democracy, the less the successes it has had to report, and the more one critically examines that prescription, the greater it is contradicted by the colonial and postcolonial histories of unequal relations between Africa and the prescribing West .

Even the most optimistic of African journalists would hesitate to term liberal democracy and Africa good bedfellows. If African journalists were to scrutinize beyond minimalism the democratization projects with which they've been involved since the early 1990s for example, they'd agree that implementing liberal democracy in Africa has been like trying to force onto the body of a full-figured person, rich in all the cultural indicators of health Africans are familiar with, a dress made to fit the slim, de-fleshed hollywood consumer model of a Barbie doll-type entertainment icon. They would also agree, that together with others, instead of blaming the tiny dress or its designer, the tradition amongst journalists has been to fault the popular body or the popular ideal of beauty, for emphasizing too much bulk, for parading the wrong sizes, for just not being the right thing.

Not often have African journalists questioned the experience and expertise of the liberal democracy designer or dressmaker, nor his/her audacity to assume that the parochial cultural palates that inform his/her peculiar sense of beauty should play God in the lives of Africa and African cultures.

In Africa, the history of difficulty at implementing liberal democracy and the role of journalism therein attests to this clash of values and attempts to ignore African cultural realities that might well have enriched and domesticated liberal democracy towards greater relevance. By overstressing individual rights and underplaying the rights of communities (cultural, religious and otherwise), African Journalism and the liberal democracy it has uncritically endorsed, have tended to be more of liabilities than assets to the aspirations for recognition and for a voice by the very Africans and communities they target. yet, given the fact that Africans (journalists included) in their daily lives continue to emphasise relationships and solidarities over the illusion of autonomy, it is difficult to imagine the future direction of democracy outside a marriage or conviviality between individual aspirations and community interests, especially in a context where whole groups were, under colonialism and apartheid, dispossessed not as individuals, but as racial, ethnic and cultural groups, imagined or real.

Thus, for democracy and journalism to succeed in the present postcolonial context of the 21st century, their proponents must recognise the fact that most Africans (and indeed everyone else) are primarily patriotic to their home village (region, province, ethnic, cultural community, etc), to which state and country in the postcolonial sense are only secondary. It is in acknowledging and providing for the reality of individuals who, like Barack Obama, negotiate and navigate different forms of identity and belonging, and who are willing or forced to be both 'citizens' and 'subjects', that democracy stands its greatest chance in Africa and the world, and that journalism can best be relevant to all and sundry in Africa and beyond.

Despite the tendency to distinguish between what mahmood mamdani has termed 'citizens and subjects' in scholarly circles, in Africa (and indeed everywhere else at a closer look), we find individuals who are both citizens and subjects, who straddle 'cultural' and 'civic' citizenships, but who would not accept sacrificing either permanently. Sometimes they are more the one than the other and sometimes more the other than the one, but certainly not reducible to either. They appropriate both in the most creative and fascinating ways. A democracy or journalism that focuses too narrowly on the individual and is insensitive to the centrality of group and community interests is likely to impair and frustrate the very recognition and representation it celebrates. It pays to go beyond prescriptions to describe the lives of actually individuals seeking to make sense of the competing and often conflicting demands of on them as social beings.

Regardless of the status of those involved in 'rights talk' and 'culture talk', they all are convinced of one thing: 'cultural citizenship' is as integral to democracy as political and economic citizenship, irrespective of how they came by their cultural identities. If African (or marginal) philosophies of personhood and agency stress interdependence between the individual and the community and between communities, and if journalists each identify with any of the many cultural communities all seeking recognition and representation at local, national and global levels, they are bound to be torn between serving their cultural communities and serving the 'imagined' rights-bearing, autonomous individual 'citizen' of the liberal democratic civic model. A democracy that stresses independence, in a situation where both the worldview and the material realities emphasise interdependence, is bound to result only in dependence.

The liberal democratic rhetoric of rights dominated by a narrow neo-liberal focus on 'The Individual', does not reflect the whole reality of personhood and agency in Africa (imagined and related to as marginal), which is a lot more complex than provided for in liberal democratic prescription of rights and empowerment. Instead of working for a creative mix with indigenous forms of politics and government, liberal democracy has sought to replace these, posing as the One-Best-Way of modern democratic political organisation, the right way of conducting modern politics, yet failing to de-marginalise Africa enough to fulfil its prescriptions. So also has the journalism it inspires, stayed narrow and asphyxiating to alternative outlooks and practices of sharing news and information, and of entertaining and educating.

In the use of language alone, few African journalists have dared to write the way Chinua Achebe suggests is a popular mode of communication amongst the Igbo, where proverbs are the palm oil with which words are eaten. Fewer still have dared to contemplate using English, French, Portuguese or Spanish the creative ways that the ordinary Africans whom they purportedly target with their journalism do. While journalists mark time with linguistic orthodoxy, African communities have been busy creolizing inherited European languages through promoting intercourse with African languages, and in turn enriching local languages through borrowings. Everywhere the spoken word has also perfected its intermarriage with the unspoken through body language and other nonverbal forms. And with the introduction of the cell phone, instant and SmS messaging, the youth are adding onto such creativity through their innovative use of language codes to communicate with one another.

When African journalists begin to reflect such popular creativity among Africans, and without a sense of guilt that they are violating journalistic taboos, they would be helping towards a democracy and journalism of relevance to, in and on Africa. In this, there is much in how Africans relate to their cultures and home village to inspire African journalists. Instead of seeing it as a problem to be defined out of the realm of acceptability, African Journalism must recognise and provide for the fact that, the home village in Africa has retained its appeal both for those who have been disappointed by the town, as well as for those who have found success in the town. It takes going beyond prescriptiveness to capture the lives of urbanites and villagers to see the relationships and practices that link them, making of them navigators and negotiators of multiple spaces and identity margins.

Recognising indigenous African forms should not be mistaken for throwing the baby of adaptability out with the bathwater. African popular musicians for example have evolved and continue to develop musical idioms that capture ongoing processes by Africans at modernising their cultures and traditionalising their modernities. Indeed, the mechanisms developed by Africans in response to the above scenarios are complex, fascinating and informed by ideas of personhood and agency that simply refuse to be confined to the logic of, dichotomies, essentialism, the market and profitability, as the rich personal account of one of Africa's leading contemporary musicians, manu Dibango, demonstrates. As an African musician who has lived the best part of his professional life in Paris and whose music has been enriched by various encounters, manu Dibango describes himself as "Négropolitain", "a man between two cultures, two environments", whose music cannot simply be reduced to either, without losing part of his creative self (Dibango 1994:88-130).

It appears that no one is too cosmopolitan to be local as well. We only have to note the creative ways Africans have harnessed the cell phone to interlink town and home village, to know how disinterested in a culture of winner-takes-all Africans are. Faced with the temporality or transience of personal success in the context of African modernities, even the most achieving and cosmopolitan of individuals hesitate to sever their rural connections entirely. The city and the 'world out there' brought closer by accelerated mobility and interconnections are perceived as hunting grounds; the home village is the place to return at the end of the day. Investing in one's home village is generally seen as the best insurance policy and a sign of ultimate success, for it guarantees survival even when one has lost everything in the city and abroad, and secures and makes manifest a realisation of success through satisfying obligations and fulfilling requests.

Thus, although successful urbanites may not permanently return or retire to the rural area as such, most remain in constant interaction with their home village through all sorts of ways. Some leave express instructions with kin to be buried or re-buried in their home village. Prescriptive journalism that denounces this reality instead of understanding, adapting and relating to it, is bound to be a liability to Africans and their ways of life. The narrow insistence on individual rights and freedoms has thus impaired understanding of the interconnectedness of peoples, cultures and societies through individuals as products, negotiators and creative manipulators or navigator of multiple identities.

Discussing democracy and journalism in Africa calls for scrutiny of the importance of cultural identities in the lives of individuals and groups. This argument challenges reductionist views of democracy and journalism, acknowledges the fact that democracy and journalism may take different forms, and most particularly, that they are construed and constructed differently in different societies, informed by history, culture and economic factors.

The way forward is in recognising the creative ways in which Africans merge their traditions with exogenous influences to create realities that are not reducible to either but enriched by both. The implication of this argument is that how we understand the role of African Journalism depends on what democratic model we draw from.

Under liberal democracy where the individual is perceived and treated as an autonomous agent, and where primary solidarities and cultural identities are discouraged in favour of a national citizenship and culture, journalism is expected to be disinterested, objective, balanced and fair in gathering, processing and disseminating news and information. The assumption is that since all individuals have equal rights as citizens, there can be no justification for bias among journalists. But under popular notions of democracy where emphasis is on interdependence and competing cultural solidarities are provided for, journalists and the media are under constant internal and external pressure to promote the interests of the various groups competing for recognition and representation.

The tensions and pressures are even greater in situations where states and governments purport to pursue liberal democracy in principle, while in reality they continue to be highhanded and repressive to their populations. When this happens, journalists are at risk of employing double- standards as well, by claiming one thing and doing the opposite, or by straddling various identity margins, without always being honest about it, especially if their very survival depends on it.

To democratise means to question basic monolithic assumptions, conventional wisdom about democracy, journalism, government, power myths and accepted personality cults, and to suggest and work for the demystification of the state, custom and society. To democratize African Journalism is to provide the missing cultural link to current efforts, links informed by respect for African humanity and creativity, and by popular ideas of personhood and domesticated agency. It is to negotiate conviviality between competing ideas of how best to provide for the humanity and dignity of all and sundry. It is above all to observe and draw from the predicaments of ordinary Africans forced by culture, history and material realities to live their lives as 'subjects' rather than as 'citizens', even as liberal democratic rhetoric claims otherwise. The mere call for an exploration of alternatives in African Journalism, is bound to be perceived as a threat and a challenge.

In particular, such a call would receive a hostile hearing from those who have championed the cause of one-dimensionalism nationally and internationally – that is, those who benefit from the maintenance of the status quo, and who stand to lose from any changes in African Journalism. They cannot withstand the challenge, stimulation and provocation that a more democratic (as the effective – as opposed to token – celebration of difference and diversity) journalism promises. They want life to go on without disturbance or fundamental change, especially by or in favour of those at the margins. And they are well placed to ensure this, thanks to their power to define and regulate journalism, the power to accord or to deny a voice to individuals and communities.

Only well-articulated policies informed by public interest broadly defined to include individual and community expectations, and scrupulously respected, would guarantee against such abuse and misuse of office and privilege. The future of democracy and the relevance of journalism to Africans and their predicaments will depend very much on how well Africans are able to negotiate recognition and representation for their humanity and creativity beyond the tokenism of prevalent politically correct rhetoric on equality of humanity and opportunity.

Journalism, to be relevant to social consolidation and renewal in Africa, must embrace professional and social responsiveness in tune with the collective aspirations of Africans. In a context where economic and political constraints have often hindered the fulfilment of this expectation, the advent and increasing adoption in Africa of ICTs offer fascinating new possibilities. While journalists are usually open to new technologies in their work, their practice of journalism has not always capitalized upon the creative ways in which the public they target for and with information adopt, adapt and use the very same technologies. The future for democracy and the relevance of journalism therein would have much to learn from the creative ways in which Africans are currently relating to innovations in ICTs. The same popular creativity that has been largely ignored by conventional journalism in the past is remarkable today all over Africa and amongst Africans in the Diaspora. The body of literature informed by empirical research is considerable to suggest that individuals and the cultural communities they represent often refuse to celebrate victimhood. They seek to harness, within the limits of the structural constraints facing them, whatever possibilities are available to contest and seek inclusion. hence the need to highlight the importance of blending conventional and citizen journalism through the myriad possibilities offered by ICTs to harness both democracy and its nemesis. The current context of globalization facilitated by the ICTs offers exciting new prospects not only for citizens and journalists to compete and complement one another, but also an opportunity for new solidarities to challenge undemocratic forces, ideologies and practices that stand in the way of social progress.

Thus, although Internet connectivity in Africa is lowest compared to other areas of the world, Africa's cultural values of sociality, interconnectedness, interdependence and conviviality make it possible for others to access the Internet and its opportunities without necessarily being connected themselves. In many situations, it suffices for a single individual to be connected for whole groups and communities to benefit. The individual in question acts as a point of presence or communication node, linking other individuals and communities in a myriad of ways and bringing hope to others who would otherwise be dismissed as not belonging by capital and its excessive emphasis on the autonomous individual consumer.

In parts of the continent where resident telephone lines are grossly inadequate and defective at best, and where Internet connections are difficult and expensive, literate and illiterate people eager to stay in touch with relations, friends and opportunities within and in the Diaspora flood the few Internet points with messages to be typed and emailed on their behalf. Replies to their emails are printed out, addressed and pigeonholed for them by the operators who cannot afford to check for mails regularly because of exorbitant costs. What is noteworthy, however, is that the high charges do not seem to temper the determination of those involved to stay in touch with the outside world.

Through such connections, people are able to exchange news on family, projects, events and developments of a personal and general nature. They are also able to exchange news on different cultural products and to arrange on how to acquire the products for one another. It is mainly through this means that many Africans abroad or in the Diaspora do not miss out on local music releases, publications, satirical humour, artifacts and fashion. Each visit to the home village is armed with a long list of cultural products to take back for oneself, fellow Africans and friends. many unmarried young men and women in the Diaspora would have given up hope of marrying someone from their home village or country and doing so in accordance with local customs and traditions, had email not been there to facilitate contacts and negotiations with parents and potential families-in-law.

In addition, the cosmopolitan identities of Africans in the Diaspora personally and through websites serve as itinerant billboards or as evangelists seeking converts for the cultures of their home villages. Thanks to such advertisements and websites, marabouts, sangomas, ngangas have been drawn to the West and other centres of modern accumulation where the rising interest in the occult is creating demand and opportunities for their muti or magic from Africa. The growing need for magical interpretations to material realities under millennial capitalism has meant creating space on the margins for marginalized cultures and solutions. This would explain the back-street shops and dealers in African cultural products, ranging from foods to charms and amulets. It also explains the fact that not all the customers visiting these shops and markets are Diasporic Africans. The Diaspora and the rest of the world are thus connected to the local, and both can work actively to ensure continuity for cultures and communities marginalized at the national and global levels by the big players. Lesson: it does not have to be big to be noticed.

The same creativity displayed in relation to the Internet is true of the cell phone, which has rapidly become the new talking drum of everyday Africa. Africa has the fastest growth rate in the world for cell phones. The latest technology to be domesticated is the cell phone, which almost everywhere on the continent is being used creatively by poor urban dwellers and Diasporic Africans to stay in touch with relatives and channel remittances, and through them maintain healthy communication with the living-dead. Even those who cannot afford a cell phone stand to benefit thanks to the sociality and solidarity of the local cultures of which they are a part.

Most cell phone owners in West Africa and central Africa for example, tend to serve as points of presence for their community, with others paying or simply passing through them to make calls to relatives, friends and contacts within or outside the country. Thus although countries in these regions might actually own fewer phones than most countries in the West or elsewhere, and despite their relatively low level of economic activity relative to other parts of the world, the economic and social value of a cell phone in them as single-owner-multiple-user countries is much higher than that of a cell phone in countries with single-owner-single-user communities. Contrary to popular opinion, sociality, interdependence and conviviality are not always a obstacle to profitability.

The lessons for African journalism of such creative appropriation processes under way are obvious. Comprehending the overall development, usage and application of ICTs within African social spaces would take the fusion of keen observation and complex analysis to capture structural, gendered, class, generational, racial and spatial dimensions of the phenomenon. A dialectical interrogation of the processes involved promises a more accurate grasp of the linkages than would impressionistic, linear and prescriptive narratives of technological determinism. If African journalism pays closer attention to the creative usages of ICTs by ordinary Africans, African journalists could begin to think less of professional journalism in the conventional sense, and more of seeking ways to blend the information and communication cultures of the general public with their conventional canon and practices, to give birth to a conventional cum-citizen journalism that is of greater relevance to Africa and its predicaments.

I think "citizen journalism" brings a whole new dimension to the mainstream journalism in Africa of which I have been critical for being so neatly detached from what is really going on in the ordinary lives of people and how they make news, how they gather news and how they communicate. It is because our journalists, by sticking too narrowly and indeed hypocritically to liberal democratic normative canons of journalism, miss the point of African value added in terms of how people communicate and how they share communication with one another. And Africa has a much richer landscape in this regard that can inform journalism. Before citizen journalism became popularised, you had citizen journalism all over Africa. Ordinary people used forms such as "radio trottoir", social commentary, rumour and various other forms of political derision and art to obtain information, share it and create possibilities where normal channels were beyond their reach. So citizen journalism provides an opportunity to revisit an old problem, that of understanding popular forms of communication and how they blend in with conventional media for the best of society.

Indeed, thanks to innovations in ICT, the structure and content of the big media are being challenged and compelled to be more sensitive to cultural diversity. The very same innovations facilitate new media cultures and practices through the possibilities they offer radical, alternative, small independent, local and community media. Through their capacity for flexibility and accessibility, the ICT that make possible new media, cultural communities hitherto marginalised are better catered for even within the framework of dominance by the global cultural industries. The current advantage being taken of the ICT by cultural communities the world over seeking recognition and representation should be seen in this light, and above all, as an example from which conventional journalism draw.

De Bruin, M, Nyamnjoh, F.B. and Brinkman, I. (eds), (2009), *Mobile Phones: The New Talking Drums of Everyday Africa*, Langaa/ASC Leiden: Bamenda.

Dibango, M.(in collaboration with Danielle Rouard) (1994) *Three Kilos of Coffee: An Autobiography* (The University of Chicago Press: Chicago)

Mamdani, M., (1996), *Citizen and Subject: Contemporary Africa and the Legacy of Late Capitalism*, Cape Town: David Philip.

Mamdani, M. (ed.) (2000), *Beyond Rights Talk and Culture Talk,* Cape Town, South Africa: David Philip.

Miller, D. and Slater, D. (2000) *The Internet: An Ethnographic Approach*, Oxford : Berg. Mpe, P. (2001),

Welcome to Our Hillbrow, Pietermaritzburg, South Africa: University of Natal Press.

Nyamnjoh, F.B., (2005a), *Africa's Media, Democracy and the Politics of Belonging*, London: Zed Books.

Nyamnjoh, F.B., (2005b), 'Images of Nyongo amongst Bamenda Grassfielders in Whiteman Kontri', *Citizenship Studies*, vol.9(3):241-269.

ETHICS IN JOURNALISM: WHY AND HOW?

Christina Chan-Meetoo

"[...] mass communication is central in a democracy and in the processes of a democracy"
(Fourie, 2001)

We now live and interact in a highly mediated system. The sheer amount of information produced and distributed by the mass media on a daily basis can impact significantly on the manner in which people, communities and societies understand (or misunderstand) each other. Whether it is considered as a fourth estate, a watchdog or a pillar of democracy, the press is undoubtedly an essential element of the public sphere.

However, it continuously faces several challenges and is assailed by multiple forces. Indeed, competition on the digital front, pressures to publish fast and quick, the temptation of sensationalism, job insecurity and high staff turnover are some of the threats to the profession. The constraints abound both on the internal front (search for new revenue models, unstable recruitment and training, lack of professionalisation, conflicts of interest, ownership issues, etc.) and on the external front (government pressure, economic pressure, competition, public scrutiny, etc.).

With so many constraints, how can the news media live up to the expectations of its ever more demanding audience? As the need to demonstrate that the public can continue to believe and trust in it is more acute than ever in the age of digital openness and scrutiny, we are inevitably led back to the fundamentals of journalism. Indeed journalism must not only aim to be intrinsically truthful and honest, but also needs to actively prove its worth in the public sphere. In other words, it must demonstrate that it has a solid sense of ethics.

It is a fact that once information has found its way into the public space, it is difficult to take it back. Therefore it is imperative that those who are in the industry of information and news production are armed with the necessary skills and mechanisms to process, report and represent information along ethical lines. It must be emphasised from the onset that ethics is not the law but that its use and application help enhance the quality of journalism and push for greater responsible reporting.

A workshop on ethics in the practice of journalism was held in October 2012 in Mauritius with participants from Seychelles and Mauritius. It aimed at providing media practitioners with the necessary tools for reflecting on their trade and for ensuring that ethical considerations are always top of the agenda in the newsroom, for a healthier public sphere where accusations of unethical reporting are mitigated (and consequently attacks to freedom of the press may not be justified).

Indeed, the local media in Mauritius are often accused by political stakeholders of being biased and unprofessional. Governments conveniently use these arguments to brandish the threat of state regulation and tougher media laws. The present government regularly evokes the setting up of a Media Commission and has appointed Geoffrey Robertson QC to draft new media laws. Whilst it is true that there are many cases of unethical reporting, direct government intervention and control is certainly not warranted. This would undoubtedly represent a threat to freedom of expression and democracy in a small highly politicised country like ours. The government appointed consultant himself does not seem to be in favour of such drastic measures to address the problem. At his last conference in Mauritius in May 2012, Robertson pleaded for self-regulation and even stated that freedom of information legislation is needed in Mauritius.

It should here be noted that the preliminary report 'Media Law and Ethics in Mauritius' was presented in April 2013 by Geoffrey Robertson QC. The main proposals concerned the setting up of an Ombudsman's office, the review of defamation and sedition laws, as well as the introduction of Freedom of Information legislation.

As for Seychelles, the situation is somewhat different as it has a Media Commission since 2010. This Media Commission was set up by the National Assembly and all its members nominated by the President. As it is a rather young institution, it is difficult to say whether it is acting in a totally neutral and independent manner from government.

The problem is that, upon hearing the word "ethics", people shudder as they think it is too grand and automatically associate it with moral eugenics and conformism. While the risk exists that codes of ethics could lead to the temptation of excessive highbrow morality, this is still not a sufficient argument to simply not have any framework for a common agreement as to what is acceptable or not in the way news are sourced, treated and put into the public arena. The possible negative consequences of decisions made by news people cannot simply be overlooked and brushed aside. Just as the news media expects the other three estates (i.e. the legislative, the judiciary and the executive) to be subjected to scrutiny in the interest of the public they are supposed to serve, similarly the so-called fourth estate (i.e. the press) should also naturally agree to such scrutiny.

However, many have tried to confine ethics to the boundaries of the individual and the personal, arguing that it cannot come from without, that it cannot be imposed. The voluntary dimension of ethical practice is indeed an essential component from an ideal standpoint. However, as history has proved that leaving news media to their own devices is not a good idea, most democratic countries have adopted some form of regulation framework, ranging from statutory regulation (imposed by law) to independent self-regulation by the industry (without any state intervention). It should be noted here that state-controlled statutory regulation is not considered as desirable for the written press in most stable democracies (as opposed to broadcasting which is historically subjected to stricter regulation).

There are of course a variety of possible forms and structures for self-regulation as set out by Johan Retief (Ombudsman for the Press Council of South Africa) in the following sections. Such types of regulation are effected through well-defined and recognised instruments like codes of ethics and conduct, press councils and ombuds offices.

In Mauritius, there is neither direct state regulation nor any established and recognised self-regulation of the written press. Instead, there is currently regulation through harsh criminal laws inherited from the colonial times; laws relating to sedition, public offence, defamation, libel, false news... These are more often used by politicians than any other category of the public and are thus clearly not suitable for the protection of the mass, for people who are unable or unwilling to go to court as the legal route is generally too time-consuming, costly and complex.

We must recognise that there have been some attempts for self-regulation through the creation of codes of ethics and conduct within some news desks as well as some associations such as the defunct *Association des Journalistes Mauriciens* and the stillborn *Newspapers Editors and Publishers Association*. The issue is that few journalists seem to know the content of the above codes and obviously very few actively refer to such codes in their daily practice. More importantly, there is very little awareness among the public of the existence of such codes and thus limited possibility to interpellate the press for any breach to their own code of ethics.

One noteworthy attempt was made by the press company La Sentinelle in 2008 to set up an ethics committee comprising of an academic, a retired judge and a retired civil servant to adjudicate on complaints for non-compliance with their code. But, the effort was short-lived and showed limited transparency and results.

Though laudable, such segregated attempts to establish and promote ethical practice in journalism are clearly not sufficient.

In any case, the mere existence of one particular instrument will not necessarily lead to a totally ethical press. Codes of ethics or codes of conduct without any mechanism for monitoring and accountability do not serve any real purpose as acknowledged by Mauritian journalists themselves in a survey on ethics in journalism. 82% of the respondents believe that the profession needs a unique code and 56% think that an industry-wide regulatory mechanism is needed to impose that code.

Survey on ethics in journalism

The survey was carried out online in March 2013 with journalists and editors-in-chief in Mauritius to gauge their appreciation of ethical levels in their own profession. The qualitative method was chosen in order to allow the respondents to express their views in an elaborate manner. 34 persons from a diversity of media houses and beats responded to the online questionnaire. The anonymity of respondents was guaranteed.

From responses to the survey, there are multiple issues which need to be addressed, namely, the treatment of sordid news, the protection of children and of rape victims, conflicts of interest, publication without verification, biased coverage, separation of facts from opinion and ethnic hatred inter alia.

Where they work:

- Private radio stations
- Public radio and TV station (MBC)
- Leading dailies
- Leading weeklies
- Specialised weeklies
- Alternative media
- Experienced former journalists

Use of codes

85% of the journalists who responded claimed that they do use a code of ethics. A majority of those stated that they use a code from their own newsdesks. 5 out of 34 journalists stated that they use the NEPA code. One stated that (s)he does not use a code of ethics and instead has recourse to legal advice on a regular basis.

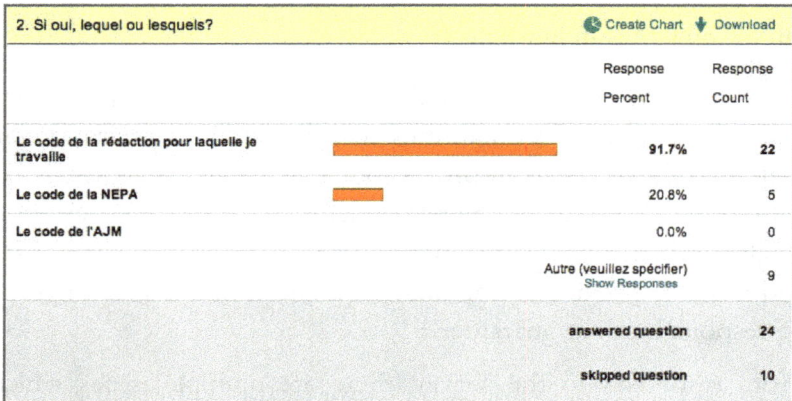

2. Si oui, lequel ou lesquels?		Create Chart ⬇ Download	
		Response Percent	Response Count
Le code de la rédaction pour laquelle je travaille		91.7%	22
Le code de la NEPA		20.8%	5
Le code de l'AJM		0.0%	0
	Autre (veuillez spécifier) Show Responses		9
	answered question		24
	skipped question		10

Code of ethics used by journalists

3. A votre avis, les codes d'éthique ou de conduite qui existent à Maurice....	Create Chart	Download		
			Response Percent	Response Count
... sont effectivement utilisés par les rédactions et les journalistes pour les guider dans leur pratique professionnelle.			33.3%	10
... ont suscité un intérêt au sein de la profession lors de leur lancement mais ont été vite oubliés car il n'y a pas de mécanisme pour leur mise en application.			53.3%	16
... ont été préparés pour jeter de la poudre aux yeux et ne servent donc à rien sinon à faire joli.			16.7%	5
		Autre (veuillez spécifier) Hide Responses		5

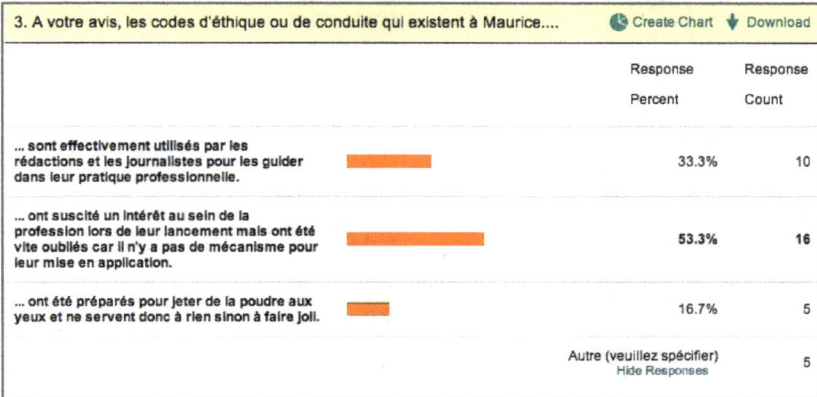

Usefulness of existing codes of ethics

Only 33% of the journalists feel that the existing codes of ethics or conduct are effectively used by journalists. Most believe that the codes attracted attention on launch but were quickly forgotten as there is no mechanism for monitoring and application (53%). A few (17%) even agreed with the statement that the codes were launched for the show and were never meant to serve any real purpose.

Responses (5)	Text Analysis	My Categories (0)
Showing 5 text responses		No responses selected

Servent de texte de référence qu'en cas de questions particulièrement compliquées.
4/2/2013 11:19 PM   View Responses

Ne sont pas bien connus ni vulgarisés
4/2/2013 8:20 PM   View Responses

Non par reaction a un evenement, et non par souci de professionnalisme, et donc pour se donne bonne conscience. Mais bien, les habitudes ont repris leur cour.
4/2/2013 1:02 PM   View Responses

Tout dépend du niveau de sérieux et professionnalisme des journalistes individuellement. Certains s'y référent systématiquement. D'autres consentent parfois à "oublier" les règles soit par convenance ou à cause de la pression de leurs responsables et/ou direction.
3/29/2013 4:27 PM   View Responses

ils n'ont jamais été testés et ne sont donc pas efficaces et en plus il n'y a aucune instance pour les faire appliquer donc c'est une intention incomplète.
3/29/2013 8:04 AM   View Responses

Usefulness of existing codes of ethics

4. Quelle est votre opinion sur l'éthique en journalisme en général à Maurice?	Create Chart	Download		
			Response Percent	Response Count
Excellente. Tous les journalistes ont une conscience et une pratique éthique.			0.0%	0
Bonne. La majorité des journalistes ont une conscience et une pratique éthique.			18.2%	6
Acceptable. Une partie des journalistes ont une conscience et une pratique éthique.			45.5%	15
Mauvaise. Très peu de journalistes ont une conscience et une pratique éthique.			27.3%	9
Exécrable. Aucun journaliste n'a une conscience ni une pratique éthique.			9.1%	3
			answered question	33
			skipped question	1

Opinion on level of ethics in journalism

Not a single respondent believes that the level of ethics in journalism in Mauritius is excellent but most feel that it is acceptable (46%) and good (18%). 36% feel the level is bad, even mediocre.

Ethical issues faced by journalists

When asked about personal experience with ethical issues, half of the respondents stated that they have either witnessed or been personally confronted with incidents involving an ethical dimension. One stated that (s)he currently has a case in court without providing further information about the case.

A few were very critical of their own news organisations which encourage unethical behaviour to provide sensationalist content so as to sell more papers, indulge in disinformation and publish unverified information. Some cited the influence of the newspaper's corporate owners who tried to mitigate coverage of scandals linked to their banking activity, linkages of news editors to some harmful organisations or external pressure to refrain from covering sensitive news about powerful political figures. Other ethical dilemmas concerned PR gifts, offer of rewards from those whose lives had been changed after positive coverage and requests to view texts before publication. The case of the MBC was also evoked with its completely partisan coverage of parliamentary debates and cover up of scandals involving political figures.

Their views on ethics in journalism in Mauritius

Most journalists feel that there is lack of objectivity in the profession (44%), especially in propagandist media organs associated with the ruling party but also within more so-called independent publications and radio stations which do not always separate fact from opinion and even indulge in partisan coverage of political events and issues. Many are also shocked by the sensationalist coverage of crime and sex stories, specially the use of explicit headlines and pictures involving sexual aggression (32%) and the publication of crude photos of cadavers and accidents (32%). 12% are disturbed by coverage which involves innocent minors who are identified by name or photography. Other cases evoked include the publication of unverified information, irresponsible journalism inciting people to break the law and recording without permission.

The majority of respondents believe that a unique code ethics is very important for the whole profession in Mauritius (82%) with 56% stating that there should also be a single regulation agency such as a press council or ombuds office. A few believe that internal mechanisms for each media house (such as a committee or ombudsperson) would be sufficient (21%). Only five journalists believe that ethics cannot be codified and two journalists stated that there should be regulation by a state agency.

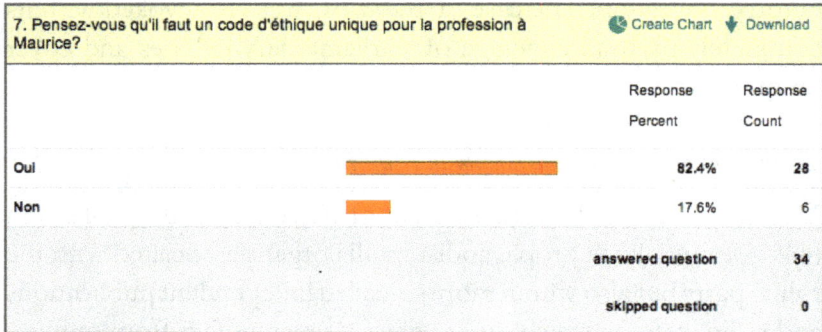

7. Pensez-vous qu'il faut un code d'éthique unique pour la profession à Maurice?		Create Chart	Download
		Response Percent	Response Count
Oui		82.4%	28
Non		17.6%	6
		answered question	34
		skipped question	0

Need for a unique code of ethics in journalism

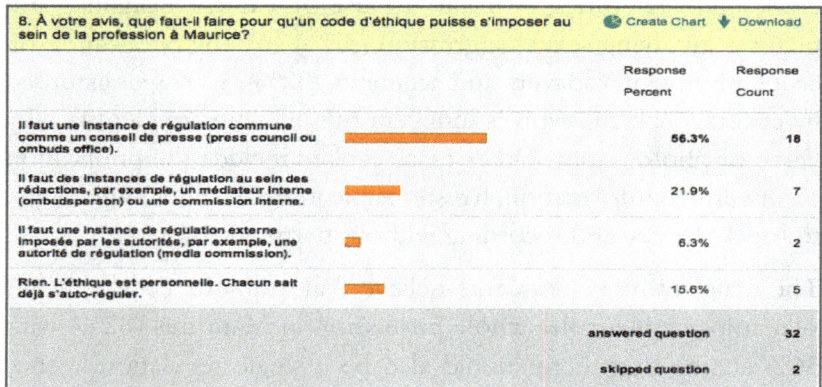

8. À votre avis, que faut-il faire pour qu'un code d'éthique puisse s'imposer au sein de la profession à Maurice?		Create Chart	Download
		Response Percent	Response Count
Il faut une instance de régulation commune comme un conseil de presse (press council ou ombuds office).		56.3%	18
Il faut des instances de régulation au sein des rédactions, par exemple, un médiateur interne (ombudsperson) ou une commission interne.		21.9%	7
Il faut une instance de régulation externe imposée par les autorités, par exemple, une autorité de régulation (media commission).		6.3%	2
Rien. L'éthique est personnelle. Chacun sait déjà s'auto-réguler.		15.6%	5
		answered question	32
		skipped question	2

Need for a single regulation framework

The state of journalism in Mauritius

Most journalists are unsatisfied with the state of journalism in Mauritius (51%) with many of the respondents providing a very harsh evaluation of the state of journalism in Mauritius. They are unhappy about manipulation, bias, propaganda, economic pressure, political pressure, sensationalism, low standards, lack of training and national television.

31% have a somewhat positive to positive appreciation of the level as they feel that the overall level is good and journalism is playing an important role in our democracy. The rest (18%) have mixed feelings as they are happy about some aspects of the local media while being critical about other major aspects.

The table below lists the key points which were raised by the respondents (translated from French):

The somewhat positive
• Journalism is good in Mauritius though it has no sense of direction.
• Newspapers and radio stations are doing a good job.
• Still some way to go to give its due to journalism in society.
• Broadsheets have good ethical level but tabloids are rather cheap.
• Important role as watchdog in a democracy though constrained by economic and commercial objectives.

The issues
- No real freedom.
- Prevalence of manipulation and bias.
- Journalists themselves are under influence.
- Hypocrisy about ethics. Some who claim to be ethics experts are themselves unethical editors who tailor news to lure and accommodate advertisers.
- Economic and political influence: self-censorship so as not to displease private advertisers as well as government agencies which place a lot of adverts in the media.
- Independent journalism (independence from government and advertising) is cornered.
- Too much focus on politics and dictated by politics.
- Hidden agendas.
- Lack of consensus for self-regulation.
- Increase in sensationalism.
- Lack of investigative journalism
- Lack of training and sensitisation about ethics.
- Level of general knowledge is low among young recruits.
- Very low level due to lack of culture, training and curiosity within the different generations of reporters.
- Lack of knowledge about history and ability to understand social issues and processes.
- Intellectual laziness.
- Lack of knowledge about laws.
- Young journalists left to their own devices are quickly overwhelmed by proximity with power circles and do not really seek information and truth.
- Turnover is too high due to low salary which does not retain those who have good potential. Media owners have big responsibility.
- Experienced journalists are fired or not replaced when they retire. Young journalists are not given any coaching.
- New consumption patterns by young readers.
- Mauritius is like dictatorships when it comes to television. State TV is like a dinosaur which only carries governmental propaganda.

> **The Mixed feelings**
>
> - There's the good, the bad and the ugly in the profession like everywhere else in the country (population and politicians included).
> - Extremely different levels of excellence and professionalism versus amateurism and mediocrity.

> **The Challenges**
>
> - Need to reinvent journalism due to democratisation of journalism (internet).
> - Need for private TV.

When going through the responses of the journalists, one can see that they have a rather lucid assessment of the importance of their profession, the systemic constraints and the impending challenges. They themselves feel that there is an urgent need for a unique code of ethics and a monitoring / enforcement agency so that the code does not remain a mere sham. They however want to stave off government control and ensure real independence from all undue influences, whether political or economic.

The need for a unique code and a regulation mechanism

Codes are documents that are useful in pinning down the tenets of good journalism practice, just like other sectors which have a strong linkage with the public sphere (e.g. lawyers, police force, civil service). Codes of ethics or conduct do provide a reference for acceptable behaviour but they should ideally be adopted after consultation with the public, with regular updates to respond to the needs of the day. Which is far from being the case here. Also, once the codes are adopted, compliance has to be ensured so that they do not remain as mere window-dressing actions.

This can only be ensured through formal mechanisms such as strong internal ombudspersons and commissions or industry-wide press councils and ombuds offices. The institution of a proper body to oversee the formulation, implementation and monitoring of the code of ethics and its application is much needed. Although the Media Trust recommended the setting up of a press council in 1998 through the Kenneth Morgan report, the industry did not agree to its implementation and the organisation itself has been hijacked by the government[1].

As a result, we have an unfortunate situation where the State and the press are constantly at daggers' end with regular threats of tough media laws on the one hand and insidious partisan political reporting on the other. The public is a mere standby witness of the feud and its members often are helpless victims of unethical, biased, sensationalist reporting. But how can we ensure that there is strong regulation that is neither tampered with by politicians nor confiscated by the self interests of the industry?

In Mauritius, the models to which we tend to turn our gaze are often France and the United Kingdom, our former colonial masters. As Bruno Albin, former senior journalist in France explains in this book, there is no industry-wide self-regulation in his country despite the wish of the media workers' unions. There are well-known codes and charters but these are deemed insufficient for preventing journalistic scandals such as the outrageous sensationalist treatment of the Outreau case and the fake Fidel Castro interview.

As for the UK, the Press Complaints Commission seems to have failed spectacularly. The case of the scandalous methods used by the tabloid *News of the World* in the UK for sourcing and spicing up their news immediately comes to mind. The Leveson Inquiry has in fact concluded in November 2012 that it is desirable to review the present self-regulation structure in order to create a new standards body backed by legislation for a tougher independent regulator.

---

1 The Media Trust was created in 1994 through an Act. Its aims are to promote the media by providing training in the form of seminars, conferences and workshops. It has been rendered inoperative in 2006 as the government did not appoint the chairperson despite elections having been held.

Rather than try to emulate eurocentric models, we may as well examine some of the self-regulation models from our own continent: Botswana, Malawi, South Africa, Tanzania and Zambia. The one presented by Johan Retief comes from South Africa, a young democracy like ours. It is one of independent co-regulation, that is, it involves public and industry participation on a parity system, and it does not allow for government interference. A model certainly worth exploring.

References

- Bussiek, Hendrik. (2008). Self-Regulation of the Media in the SADC Region. FES Media.

- Chan-Meetoo, Christina. (2011). State or Self Regulation: The Search for Common Ground. Mauritius: UNESCO/ UOM.

- Fourie, Peter J.. (2001). Media Studies Volume 1: Institutions, Theories and Issues.Juta and Company Ltd.

- Krüger, Franz. (2009). Media Courts of Honour Self-regulatory Councils in Southern Africa and elsewhere. FES Media.

- Leveson Inquiry: Culture, Practices and Ethics of the Press, 29 November 2012.

- Morgan, Kenneth. (1998-99). A Press Council for Mauritius? Consultancy Report for the Media Trust.

- Robertson, Geoffrey. (2013). Media Law and Ethics in Mauritius. A Preliminary Report.

GUIDELINES FOR ETHICAL JOURNALISM – AND BEYOND

Johan Retief

'A Press Code is an ethical compass without
which journalists are all at sea...'

There is hardly anything that anyone can do without influencing somebody else; there is *nothing* that a journalist can do without affecting somebody – or everybody.

I often wonder if journalists really understand and appreciate just how much power they have. *Everything* they do in their professional lives influences people. This is the first thing that good journalists should realise – they have this uncanny power to effect changes in people's lives, which can either be for the better or for the worse. All too often reporters are not conscious of the fact that their influence can hardly be neutral.

I would like to believe that all journalists would rather positively, and not negatively, influence their readers. This is why media ethics is so important, as it enables one to be a constructive force, and not a destructive one – journalists can easily cause unnecessary harm to people and needlessly destroy their lives.

However, this issue is rather more complicated, as the press is not a charity or a religious organisation. Its main purpose is not to do either good or bad, but rather to report news truthfully, accurately and fairly – and if that results in either good or bad to whoever may be concerned, then so be it.

In other words, its influence is good *if it does its job properly* – whether or not it causes people harm. If, for instance, a publication exposes a corrupt politician, the consequences for that person will be bad, but for the rest of society it will be good.

In this book I shall try to help journalists to be ethical in their work. In this process, I shall start with a brief theoretical session on media ethics. I shall then discuss self-regulation and how this is done in South Africa, before I'll proceed to the South African Press Code and its implications. I'll end off with more practicalities, and with official texts.

I believe that a practical approach is best, which is why I limit the theoretical discussion as much as I can – this would be more helpful to the industry than a pure academic approach.

I am convinced that many institutions that teach media ethics (or at least most of those that I have visited) misunderstand their task. They namely teach media ethical *theory* for most of the time, and give little or no attention to the *implementation* of those theories. That is not helpful! They should in the first place not try to produce *media ethicists* (which indeed would be an unexpected bonus), but rather try to yield *journalists* who are capable of making good ethical decision for the right reasons.

Most certainly am I not going to fall in that trap.

Note that, as Press Ombudsman, I write against the background of the printed press. In South Africa, the press (newspapers and magazines) is regulated separately from the electronic media (radio and television), which is done by the Broadcasting Complaints Commission of South Africa (the BCCSA).

I am also cognisant of the fact that Mauritius has no national regulation or a national Code – a situation that I need to address as I go along. So, if this book can be of any help to the press in Mauritius and indeed elsewhere in Africa (or even wider, for that matter), I'd be more than grateful.

I am going to discuss the South African situation not because I believe that this system is the be-all and end-all of all press regulation (no system is perfect), but rather because it indeed represents an excellent example of how the press can be regulated – which is many a damn sight better than no regulation at all.

Media Ethics

If journalists don't understand what media ethics is and how it works, they are bound to wreak havoc – as I have seen over and over again as Press Ombudsman. So, firstly, what is it? I can more easily explain what media ethics is by taking one step back – to *morality*.

Unlike the rest of nature, humans are moral beings. "Morality" (from the Latin word "moralitas", which means manner, character, proper behaviour) has to do with choices that people make to differentiate between what is "right" and what is "wrong" (right: read *principles*), and what is "good" and what is "bad" (read: *consequences*).

People make moral choices every day – but normally without even realising that they are doing so. But the matter is not so simple. Here are some intricacies:

- Sometimes principles are at loggerheads with one another (but not always);

- There can also be some tension between various possible consequences (but not in all instances); and

- Just to complicate things even more, there can be tension between (sometimes conflicting) principles and consequences (but again, not necessarily so).

Let me give an everyday example to simplify things. Imagine that your young child was naughty. You realise that you probably need to do something about it (principle: you are the parent, and therefore you should take responsibility for your child's upbringing). Here are some of the questions that may flow through your mind: Do I punish the child or not (another principle)? What will happen if I do and what will happen if I don't (there may be some conflicting consequences)? If I do, what kind of punishment is appropriate (both principles and consequences, and possibly some tension between the two)? If there are such tensions, the question then arises as to what sort of golden mean between these issues can be arrived at.

The basic moral question is: What is right and what is good in this circumstance? These are value judgements that may vary from person to person – nobody ever said that morality is an easy exercise. So that is morality. This brings me to *ethics* (from the Greek word "ethos" which means "character", just as morality does).

Right, but keep in mind that ethics has since developed into a conscious reasoned social *science*. Ethics and morality are indeed identical, with the exception that ethics bring moral decisions *consciously*, *reasoned* and *methodically* to the fore.

It becomes a science, as it:

- sets itself a goal (to determine what is right and wrong, and what is good and bad – and to find a golden mean if there is any tension somewhere);

- uses a method (basically using a Press Code, but also other measures – which I shall discuss later);

- reaches a result; and

- then comes to a reasoned conclusion.

Therefore: *Media Ethics* is a conscious, reasoned and methodical journalistic exercise that asks about principles (right or wrong) and consequences (good or bad), and come to a conclusion based on the result of this reasoning; and if there is some tension somewhere, it tries to determine what kind of golden mean would be appropriate.

In simpler terms: Media Ethics tries to establish what is right and good in journalism, and how to attain it. It is only when journalists consciously and methodically take this road that they would have a chance to report ethically and therefore do their job properly.

In this book I shall attempt to make this theory relevant by showing how media ethics can be put into practice. In the meantime, here are some examples of rather complicated media ethical decisions.

A South African artist once exhibited a portrait of President Jabob Zuma in the nude, with his vital parts clearly visible. The background to this painting was that Zuma had four wives and also that he had been involved in a rape trial (which he won). He was also notorious for saying that he had taken a shower after he had had sex (with the same woman who accused him of rape) in order to make sure that he did not get infected by HIV/AIDS.

The point is not the painting itself – that was a work of art which is not under discussion here. The question was how publications should have covered the matter, if at all.

So, these were the media ethical questions that the press (consciously) had to respond to: What principles were involved? Was there any conflict between these principles? Surely, in this case the right to freedom of expression (principle) had to be weighed up against the right to dignity and privacy (another principle). Moreover, did the fact that Zuma was Head of State give him a greater right to dignity and privacy than ordinary citizens would have had (principle)? So yes, there was indeed some tension between principles.

There were also conflicting consequences: What would it have done to the robustness of the debate if the press did not cover the matter at all? If coverage should take place, consider the consequences regarding which type of reporting you were going to engage in. How would it affect him and his family – and how would his supporters react?

Thirdly, if you chose for freedom of expression, there surely would have been tension between your choice for this principle and the consequences that it was bound to have.

Another question: Was it in the public interest to cover this issue? So, in the midst of all these tensions clearly a golden mean had to be found (if you did not decide to go outright for one or the other principle).

Most publications indeed went for a golden mean – they decided to cover the event (opting for the right of freedom of expression), but simultaneously (because of the dire consequences that this may have had) covered up Zuma's vital parts.

One newspaper, however, went for the full Monty on its website. The consequences were indeed dire. Some of Zuma's supporters threatened to burn the gallery and to boycott the newspaper. One vandal ripped up the painting. In the end, the newspaper backed off, apologised and removed the picture from its website.

Now, I am not going to deliver judgment here. You decide for yourself. I merely need to point out just how difficult media ethics can be and how it can operate.

Here is another example: You discover that the town's mayor has an affair with his/her secretary. The first question is a principled one – is this a mere private matter, or should the public know about it?

This is a difficult one! Should you cover the matter in the name of freedom of expression, or should you rather uphold the mayor's dignity and reputation? Would it be in the public interest to know about the affair? If yes, why would that be? And if no, why would that be?

You also ask what the effect would be on the mayor if you do report the matter. Clearly, it could end his/her career and his/her marriage. For argument's sake, the mayor has done an excellent job and s/he has pulled the town out of the fire. Do you really want this mayor to resign?

So now you are now also considering the consequences – not only for the parties involved, but also for the whole of society. Again, the answer to this question will vary from journalist to journalist. The one journalist may report the mayor's affair, while the other may decide to ignore it (both basing their decision on the principle of public interest, or the lack thereof – and of possible consequences). In this specific case, the consequences for the publication and the journalist are not so important.

There are instances, however, where reporting indeed may have (dire) consequences for journalists. For example, a South African TV journalist once revealed sensitive information, based on data that two anonymous sources gave him. Section 205 of the Criminal Procedure Act stipulated that the state may force a journalist to reveal her or his sources – or else s/he may go to jail. The outcome of this matter is not important here. The point is that in some cases journalist should also consider the consequences of their reporting for themselves as well as for their publications.

One last example: When former USA President Bill Clinton was accused of having an affair with Ms Monica Lewinsky, this debate was rife – and not all journalists agreed with one another. The one argument was that the alleged affair was a personal matter and that the issue should therefore be ignored; other journalists felt that, if the president could be unfaithful to his wife, he could be disloyal to his job as well – and therefore the matter should be reported. The question of principles, consequences and a golden mean again came to the fore.

In complicated cases like these, there never are clear-cut answers – only responses that have hopefully been made in a responsible (read: sound media ethical) way. But do not despair – *as long as you consciously and methodically put these issues on your desk, use your media ethical "tools", and base your reasoned decisions on the outcome of your deliberations.*

Why is media ethics important?

The answer to this question is simple: The press has the (frightening) power to make or to break people, and even the whole of society; likewise, the press can play a pivotal role in building and maintaining a healthy society (because of this very power).

In other words: Media ethics is of vital importance because the press is of vital importance (because of its power); in turn the press should be taken seriously for the sake of the well-being of the whole of society. This should become clearer as we go along.

If you do not understand or believe that the press should use its power responsibly and act ethically, you may as well stop reading right here and now. And, to my mind, you should also be looking for another job – one where you cannot cause as much unnecessary harm, because you are then likely to operate like a bull in a china shop.

Press Regulation

The only way to ensure that the press understands what media ethics is and to implement it is by way of regulation.

Let me say this up-front, and this is desperately important: regulation is *not* censorship. By regulating the press, we do not mean that somebody is telling it what to write and what not – we merely recognise the fact that the press can cause huge unnecessary harm and that there is a need for a mechanism to rectify matters that have gone wrong. This means that the regulatory body should never act in advance of publication (censorship), but always only afterwards.

The need for (self-)regulation

Any democracy needs a healthy, independent Fourth Estate (read: the media – the first three estates being the legislature, the executive and the judiciary). This means that the press should act as a watchdog over the forces that shape society (see the preamble to the Press Code below). However, the question is: Should the watchdog not also be watched? And if so, who watches the watchdog?

The answers are simple:

- Yes, somebody should watch the watchdog – if nobody does that, the press can easily become a loose cannon, a force of destruction; and

- If an outside body regulates the press (mostly that would be politicians), its very freedom is at stake because that influence will then ultimately decide for the press what good journalism is. That is why I headlined this section "The need for (self-) regulation", and not merely "The need for regulation". This is the point: *The press should watch itself.*

To be sure, regulation should always start with the individual journalist (informal regulation). Again, this is not self-censorship – it merely is an attempt by reporters to be ethical in their work and to rather avoid mistakes than to rectify them or to apologise for them later. However, more than this is needed. For proper regulation there should be a formal institution (by the press and for the press) that regulates itself.

Forms of regulation

Regulation does not mean the same to everybody.

No national regulation

In some countries such as America and France there is no national regulation – media houses mostly do this on their own. Their philosophy is that citizens can take publications to court if they do not get joy from the media houses.

However, in South Africa this does not work as court procedures take an eternity to complete; besides they are costly, and many citizens simply cannot afford to litigate. I suspect that this rings true not only for the rest of Africa, but also for many other countries across the globe.

This does not mean that it is bad when media houses have their own systems of regulation. In South Africa many such institutions have their own internal ombudsman, mostly from within their own ranks. Not only do these people handle complaints by the public, but they also act as a mentor for journalists in order to avoid mistakes. But, as I have implied, this practice should be done in conjunction with a national regulatory body. Even if internal ombudsmen are not biased, members of the public may perceive them to be. The ideal is, and remains, regulation on a national basis.

Statutory Regulation

Statutory regulation means that a government passes a law that governs press regulation. Taken to its logical conclusion, this implies that the government decides for the press what good journalism should be. This form of regulation is rare, and it seems to work only in (a few) first-world countries where democracies have been firmly established.

In South Africa the press is dead against government control, and I can understand why – the press cannot afford to ignore the possibility that politicians will misuse their power to curb the right to free expression. Our democracy is much too young to entrust politicians with this enormous responsibility. The press should not fool around with its independence and guard its (and the public's) right to freedom of expression with its life. Our very democracy depends on this.

Self-regulation

In this form of regulation the press takes full responsibility to regulate its own affairs. Normally it refuses to accept any money from outside the industry for fear that it will forfeit its independence.

In 2002 the African Union made a "Declaration of Principles on Freedom of Expression in Africa". It said: "Effective self-regulation is the best system for promoting high standards in the media."

The Media Institute of Southern Africa (Swaziland) describes self-regulation as follows:

> *"Under self-regulation the media voluntarily commit to uphold a code of ethics that they themselves draft. They establish a complaints mechanism, often called a media council or complaints commission, to which the public can complain about perceived breaches of the code. The independent council adjudicates on the complaints and decides upon appropriate remedies. The courts play no role in enforcing the code of practice. Compliance with the code is voluntary and the media does so out of a desire to secure the credibility of their profession and the trust of the public."*

I could not have put it any better. Please note the emphasis on "voluntary". The system of regulation won't work if all the main players do not pull together for the sake of the greater good – even if they are as far apart from each other as the east and the west in their political and ideological opinions.

In that case, the press should get its priorities right. It would be a sad day if such differences stand in the way of voluntary regulation on a national basis. This will mean that media ethics will suffer – to the detriment of all concerned, the country's democracy included. *The press owes it to society to regulate itself* for the sake of the greater good.

In 2007 the New Zealand Press Council undertook a comprehensive study of press regulation world-wide and found that 86% of Press Councils were non-statutory (read: they had some form of self-regulation). This percentage should be 100%, as far as I am concerned.

Independent Co-regulation

This model is quite unique and has recently been implemented in South Africa. In the old South Africa (before 1994) the press was regulated by the (largely minority) Apartheid Government. For obvious reasons, this system had little or no credibility with the vast majority of the population.

After political liberation, the main press players came together and vouched not to be regulated by politicians ever again. So they opted for a system of voluntary self-regulation – and the new Government was open enough to let that be.

But boy, that openness did not last for long.

In 2012, after a period of intensive introspection and self-evaluation, triggered by the ruling party's threat of a statutory body called a Media Appeals Tribunal (MAT), the press arrived at a system that is now called "independent co-regulation". This means that regulation is independent of government, and that public participation will form 50% of the system (the press being responsible for the other 50%). This makes perfect sense, as in the end the press is accountable to the public.

Fortunately, the ruling party now seems to have accepted this (probably with a huge sigh of relief, because its MAT idea would not have passed the criteria of the South Africa Constitution in the first place).

Some media ethicists may disagree with me, but I interpret "independent co-regulation" to be a refined form of self-regulation. The point is that the press (and not anybody else) made the decision to regulate itself by sharing the process on a 50-50 basis with society. This is how the system works in South Africa.

The Press Council

The body that arose from the industry's deliberations is called the Press Council. This body is independent and is made up of six press representatives, and an equal number of public representatives. The Chief Justice recommends some judges to chair the Council, who then appoints one person from that list.

The industry chooses its own representatives. In South Africa, these are the bodies that operate: The National Editors' Forum, the Magazine Publishers Association, the Newspaper Association, the Association of Independent Publishers, and the Forum of Community Journalists.

The public positions are advertised, and an Appointments Panel – headed by another judge – heads this body.

The Press Council's role is to:

- be the guardian of the Press Code
- further freedom of expression; and
- set up an office that deals with complaints against publications (newspapers and magazines).

This Council's term of office is five years.

The office consists of a Director, a Public Advocate and an Ombudsman (together with two administrative personnel).

Note that the South African press consists of more than 1 000 publications. In smaller countries such as Mauritius that have a less diversified media industry, one person can easily fulfill the roles of all three of these positions, even on a part-time basis.

That is/was the case in Namibia – and its Ombudsman even handles both the press and the electronic media. Mauritius can easily follow this model.

The Director

This person is the CEO of the Press Council's office. His/her role is to be the public face of the Council, and also to educate the press on media ethical matters. S/he therefore visits media houses, informing journalists about the Press Code and media ethics, makes public statements, writes an annual report, analyses media ethical trends, etc.

The Public Advocate

When the office receives a complaint, the Public Advocate decides whether or not to entertain it. If so, s/he formulates and motivates the complaint on behalf of the complainant and negotiates with the publication for a speedy resolution. This person represents the complainant throughout the process, including possible hearings.

The Ombudsman

If the Public Advocate's attempts are not successful, the complaint goes to the Ombudsman for adjudication. This person then either makes a ruling based on papers, or decides to hold a hearing. In the case of a hearing, s/he chooses from the Adjudication Panel (see below) one person from the press and one from the public to be of assistance.

The Adjudication Panel

The Adjudication Panel consists of six press and eight public representatives. The industry appoints its six members; the Appointments Panel is responsible for those representing the public. This panel is also chaired by a retired judge (not the same one who chairs the Press Council). The role of the Adjudication Panel is to assist the Ombudsman in formal hearings, and to support the judge who presides over appeals hearings.

If at any stage one or both parties are not satisfied with the outcome, they have the right to apply for leave to appeal. The chair of the Adjudication Panel then either decides to dismiss the complaint, or to hold a hearing – in which case the chair chooses one person from the press and up to three from the public to hear the appeal

CONTENT OF REGULATION IN SOUTH AFRICA

Johan Retief

A Code is the first and most important way of regulating the press.

To me, it is unthinkable that journalists can operate without a Code of Ethics. This document should be to journalists what the Bible is to Christians or the Koran to Muslims. That is why I am going to take up so much space in discussing the Code, and also by printing it in its totality.

Editors often ask me for advice prior to publication. My first question always is: What does the Press Code say? In 99% of cases this solves the problem.

If you do not have a Code, then adopt one and strive to apply it to all difficult choices that you have to make. Also, spur on your publication to adopt one Code for all concerned – you really do not have to wait for somebody else to write a national Code or to re-invent the wheel. Of course, an own Code would be the first prize, but in the meantime you can move on.

The South African Press Code

After a body has been established to regulate the press, this regulation is implemented by the office of the Press Ombudsman, and s/he does this by way of a Press Code.

I am now going to discuss the South African Press Code section by section, explaining why the issues contained in them are important and giving examples to illustrate the principles and consequences that are involved – in the hope that this would provide basic guidelines to journalists for how to act ethically at all times.

I present the preamble and the Code in italics; my comments are in normal type.

Preamble

> *The press exists to serve society.*

Have you ever wondered just why you are a journalist?

The Press Council quite deliberately put this sentence up front. Journalists should be in the industry for the right reason – the arrow should always point away from reporters, and towards society. There may be many valid reasons that do point towards journalists, yes, but these reasons should always be secondary.

Journalism is not about journalists; it is about society. The serving of society ties up with another fundamental issue – the matter of accountability. Journalists are in the first instance accountable to society; only then they are also accountable to their publications.

Once journalists have grasped these fundamental truths, they would be more likely to act ethically and less prone to causing people unnecessary harm – a vital issue that I have already touched on and that I'll soon address in more detail.

> *Its freedom provides for independent scrutiny of the forces that shape society, and is essential to realising the promise of democracy.*

The press is not called the Fourth Estate for nothing. Remember what Lord Acton said: "Power corrupts, and absolute power corrupts absolutely." If there is no proper – independent and free – watchdog, politicians are likely to simply run rife and harm the very society that they (and journalists) should care for.

This is the point: Any healthy democracy is (at least partly) dependent upon the freedom of the press; without this freedom, democracy will not come to fruition – the press should therefore *independently* and *freely* scrutinise the forces that shape society in order to curtail unbridled power and abuse. It is the Press Council's task to promote this independence and freedom.

Many politicians do not like a free press, and for good reasons (seen from their perspective). At best, some of them merely tolerate it as they know how important the Fourth Estate is to their democracy. But believe you me, they are also oh so scared that the press may expose them for what they have done or are doing.

Do not be alarmed at this tension, for in a healthy democracy it should always be there – as long as the tension remains healthy, and the balance does not tilt towards either side.

Also note the phrase "promise of democracy". This serves to remind us that at least South Africa's democracy should not be taken for granted and that it should always be nurtured like a new-born baby – which makes the role of an independent press all the more important.

> *It enables citizens to make informed judgments on the issues of the day, a role whose centrality is recognised in the South African Constitution.*

The role of the press is to serve society – by giving the public information that it needs to make informed decisions on the issues of the day. The phrase "informed decisions" implies that the information should be accurate, fair, in context, etc. – which is what the content of the Code is all about. The public cannot make informed decisions if it is not adequately informed.

> *Section 16 of the Bill of Rights sets out that:*

> *1. "Everyone has the right to freedom of expression, which includes:*

63

> *a) Freedom of the press and other media;*
>
> *b) Freedom to receive and impart information or ideas;*
>
> *c) Freedom of artistic creativity; and*
>
> *d) Academic freedom and freedom of scientific research.*
>
> 2. *"The right in subsection (1) does not extend to:*
>
> *a) Propaganda for war;*
>
> *b) Incitement of imminent violence; or*
>
> *c) Advocacy of hatred that is based on race, ethnicity, gender or religion, and that constitutes incitement to cause harm."*

Firstly, for our purposes the word "everyone" and the phrase "which includes freedom of the press and other media" are of vital importance here.

These imply the following:

- The right to freedom of expression is not the privilege of a selected few – it extends to everybody;

- For the press, that means that anybody can become a journalist;

- This also implies that the press is not above society, as its right to freedom of speech is founded or based on the public's right; and

- The press is indeed special as it is specifically mentioned in the Bill of Rights.

The second part of Section 16, which in fact defines hate speech, serves to remind us that not even the freedom of the press is absolute.

Note that hate speech is defined as speech that is intended to physically harm people, which is different than the intention to hurt people (their feelings). For example, if a journalist calls somebody a fool, that would be (emotionally) hurtful – but it is not intended to be (physically) harmful. Therefore, that would not amount to hate speech.

This means that the press is not allowed to commit hate speech, whereas hurtful speech is not forbidden (in its editorial comments and columns). This distinction helps to further the robustness of the debate, which is essential to a healthy democracy.

Even if this part about hate speech was not included in the Bill of Rights or the preamble to the Code, ethical journalism would in any case have dictated that the press should never intend to physically harm people.

> *The press strives to hold these rights in trust for the country's citizens; and it is subject to the same rights and duties as the individual.*

Because the press is specifically mentioned in the Bill of Rights, it strives to act as a guardian of the right to freedom of expression. Note the word "strives". This implies that the holding of the right to freedom of expression is never a goal that can be attained – it is always in process, forever something to reach for. The press should never be complacent, thinking that nothing can attack the right to freedom of speech.

At the pinnacle of this "strives to hold these rights in trust" is the Press Council, which is set up by the industry to do exactly that. This sentence also states that the press is "subject to the same rights and duties as the individual". This means that journalists do not have special privileges – again, they have the right to know not because they are reporters, but because the public has a right to know.

> *Everyone has the duty to defend and further these rights, in recognition of the struggles that created them: the media, the public and government, who all make up the democratic state.*

Firstly, the word "everybody" is operative here. It is in the first place not the press that should further the right to freedom of expression – that is each and everybody's duty.

Also note that the Press Council had quite deliberately not said that everybody has the "right" to defend these rights – it explicitly stated that it is everybody's "duty". Everybody who is part of a democratic state, including the press, *should* defend these rights to the hilt.

The reason behind this is the recognition of those who created and presently make up the democratic state. This is important, lest we forget where we come from.

> *Our work is guided at all times by the public interest, understood to describe information of legitimate interest or importance to citizens.*

The statement that the work of the press is "at all times" guided by the public interest is important, because it gives it the necessary freedom (always coupled with responsibility, of course) to report on all information that the public should legitimately know about – no matter what.

Secondly, note that the definition of "public interest" is vague and put in general terms. The Council has done this quite deliberately as this concept is not easy to define.

However, let me add that "public interest" concerns both quantity and quality:

- Quantity: The more people are affected by an event, the more it is in the public interest. That is why (for example) extreme weather is always news – because it affects nearly everybody. Conversely, there is a certain organisation in South Africa that has only one member. Its activities can hardly be described to be in the public interest.

- Quality: The more deeply people are affected by an issue, the more it will be in society's interest to know about it – especially if it concerns a public official or figure. If a prominent public official (who is being paid with public money) is corrupt, society should know about it. The more money is involved, the more necessary it becomes for the press to report it.

Also remember that there is a difference between "public interest" and "what is interesting to the public". The first can be described as "hard news", the second as "soft news". The latter is not out of bounds as it is also enshrined in the preamble to the Code (the term "legitimate interest" can be applied to both hard and soft news).

As journalists, we commit ourselves to the highest standards of excellence, to maintain credibility and keep the trust of our readers.

Firstly, the word "commit" catches the eye: A journalist's work has to do with duty, obligation, dedication, devotion. Everybody can become a journalist, because everybody has the right to freedom of speech – but not everybody becomes a good journalist. Only those reporters who are committed will be good journalists.

Note that the preamble does not ask just any kind of commitment – it requires the maximum; it speaks of the "highest" standards of excellence.

This, by the way, is a vital difference between law and ethics. Many business people understand that they should comply with the law, but in the process they are guided by the question: What is the *minimum* that I can do (and get away with)? Ethics represents quite the opposite. It asks: What is the *maximum* that I can do in order to meet my commitment? It aims at the "highest" standards, not the "lowest". Each and every journalist should strive for the maximum.

The preamble also explains that if the press is not committed to the highest standards of excellence, it will lose its credibility and in the process forfeit the trust of its readers. If that happens, you would have lost everything and might as well pack up and go home. Credibility is earned; it does not come with the package.

This means always striving for truth, avoiding unnecessary harm, reflecting a multiplicity of voices in our coverage of events, showing a special concern for children and other vulnerable groups, and acting independently.

The whole of the preamble and the Code itself is overshadowed by this sentence. Let me go to the extreme (even overboard) for a moment – if everything else is left out of the preamble and the Code is scrapped in its totality, but these sentences are retained, all will be well as this typifies the heart of the Code and of media ethics.

Strive for truth

Firstly, the preamble states that the press should "strive for truth". This sounds so obvious that the question may arise why it was necessary to say it in the first place. The naked truth is that journalists often do not strive for truth. For example, I have seen many times that reporters only take from media releases or official documents what supports their stories – and ignore the rest. I'll return to this issue later.

Note the word "strive" (for truth). This implies an acceptance of the fact that "truth" has many facets – that "my" truth may be different from "your" truth, and that "truth" is very much like a diamond – its colour depends on the angle from which you look at it. There is a lesson in this: Never be so arrogant as to believe that you possess the whole truth and to think that somebody else is wrong just because that person differs from you.

However, this does not mean that one should become complacent – it remains of the utmost importance for journalists to indeed strive to come to truth. The word "always" (strive for truth) is weighty. There should never be one moment, one instance, that a journalist can take the eye off the ball and give up the dream.

Avoid unnecessary harm

The Code also states that the press should avoid "unnecessary harm". Let me dwell on this for a moment. The reality is that the press really is in the business of harming people. For example, if a public official is found to be corrupt, it is in the public interest to reveal this as that person is paid with public money. The publication of the story is surely bound to harm this official, but that would be in the greater good of society. In that case this official deserves to be exposed and to be caused harm by the press.

In fact, these corrupt people harm themselves. The press merely reports the corruption, and therefore is only a secondary instrument in this process – that is, if the harm that the press causes is really necessary.

This is precisely the issue here. The preamble does not say that the press should never harm anybody; at stake in media ethics is that the press should not cause people *unnecessary* harm.

A vivid example that I have encountered is the effect of a story on a man who reportedly did something wrong. Not only did this cost him his job, but he also lost his wife and children. Some months later he was able to produce credible evidence that he had been innocent all along. The newspaper then apologised, but that was too late. The harm had been done.

The press has to be careful – it can so easily cause unnecessary harm. If you don't listen to the other side, if you don't verify your information, if you depend on secondary sources, if you gullibly believe an anonymous source who may have ulterior motives, if you disregard the context, if you let yourself be influenced by outside influences (etc.), you are likely to cause unnecessary harm to people.

But I am getting ahead of myself. The point is that journalists should ask themselves every time if their reporting has the potential to harm someone: Is my reporting harming that person fairly, or unfairly; am I perhaps unnecessarily causing somebody harm?

Multiplicity of voices

The preamble says that the press should reflect a multiplicity of voices, "showing a special concern for children and other vulnerable groups". This is important, not only because it helps to prevent one-sided reporting of events, but also because it assists the press to fulfil one of its most important duties, namely to give voice to the voiceless.

In practice, this means for example that when a journalist reports on women's issues, the reporter should incorporate women's views on the matter in the story. If an article is about a minority group in society, it is unthinkable that the views of those concerned would not be heard.

The preamble specifically mentions children in this regard. Perhaps they are the most vulnerable group of them all. So if your story is about child pornography (for example), get the views of children on that matter.

Act independently

I'll discuss this issue in the section that deals with it in the Press Code itself. In order to reach these goals as set out in the preamble, the following matters should be pursued:

The South African Press Code

(The numbering below follows that of the Code.)

1. Gathering of news

1.1. News should be obtained legally, honestly and fairly, unless public interest dictates otherwise.

Firstly, a general remark: This clause carries the all-important message that journalists should act ethically not only when they write their stories, but also while they are gathering their news. The point is that *everything* journalists do have ethical consequences.

Let me take an over-the-top, thumb-suck example: A well-known public figure is attacked on a sidewalk. Somebody stabs him with a knife, grabs his purse, leaves him for dead and runs off. His wife, who saw the whole brouhaha, is hysterical.

Now the journalist comes onto the scene. It would be highly unethical to shove your tape-recorder against the victim's mouth and, while he is gurgling and gasping for his last breath of air, ask him: "How does it feel to die?" Then you turn to his wife and say: "What are your last words to him going to be?"

Of course this is an absurd example, but I do need to make the point that journalists should act ethically in everything that they do – also in the way in which they gather their news. Even the way that you talk to people over the telephone, or the tone in which you write your emails, is important.

Now, "legally": A journalist once wrote a story about homeless people who got TB. So he went to the local hospital and took a picture of such a patient, without any permission from either the hospital or the patient. In South Africa that is illegal – yet the reporter went ahead anyway.

If the journalist had asked for permission and was refused, and that reporter was convinced that it was in the public interest to report the story and there was no other way to gather his information, the Code would have allowed him to do so – even if it was illegal. In this instance, however, that was not the case.

Conversely, here is an example of news that was obtained illegally, but justifiably so: An investigative TV journalist was told that members of staff at a home for the aged abused elderly people in the bathroom. The journalist then had hidden cameras installed. In this process the TV station invaded the privacy of the aged.

The journalist did record the abuses, and screened them. Clearly, it was in the public interest to do so. Needless to say, the abuses stopped, and understandably there was no litigation against the station. (In this instance, the principle of public interest out-weighed the one of privacy.)

"Honestly and fairly": Our office has had many complaints by (for example) civil servants saying that whistle blowers unjustly and unfairly (and also illegally) gave newspapers information. However, if the information was in the public interest, it did not really matter how the journalist obtained the information (if there was no other way of getting the data).

Note that there is no need to gather news dishonestly and unfairly if there is no proper public interest involved in the matter.

> *1.2. Press representatives shall identify themselves as such, unless public interest or their safety dictates otherwise.*

Sometimes, journalists obscure their identity to obtain news. That is in order, as long as there is a public interest in the matter, or their safety is at stake, and there is no other way of obtaining the information.

I once sat in a sauna. A person started telling a story, and I immediately realized that this could be big news. I had to take a quick decision – do I reveal my identity as a journalist, or do I keep quiet and listen him out?

Some reporters would have chosen for first option; others would have gone for the second one. In a split-second I decided to reveal my identity, and gave him the option to continue or not.

Was I right? You decide.

In case you are curious: He continued with his story, and I published it the very next day.

2. Reporting of News

> *2.1. The press shall take care to report news truthfully, accurately and fairly.*

Together with Art. 2.5 (that deals with asking the subject of critical reportage for comment) this clause probably is the most fundamental part of the Code – and it also is one that is commonly transgressed.

Truthfully

Another word for "truthfully" is "honestly". You may be surprised, but a journalist once told me that has sucked out of his thumb the "best" story that he has ever written. Obviously that was before I became Press Ombudsman. Fortunately he is not a journalist anymore (as far as I know). Such a "journalist" does not belong in the industry. No argument here.

I have also come across many journalists who merely wanted to further their own ideological aims – and in the process "adjusted" their news to suit their own agendas. The most common of these errors were politically motivated. Shame on them!

Enjoy this one: A journalist from a conservative (right-wing) publication (in the old South Africa) once asked his editor if he may "adjust" his facts in order to suit the newspaper's political agenda. The editor retorted: "In a news story, you present the facts – it is up to me to distort them in my editorials."

I shall discuss comment shortly, but let me emphasise at this stage that news stories should stick to facts, and that journalists should at all cost report these facts honestly.

Accurately

The be-all and end-all of all good journalism is to check, re-check, and re-re-check. Unfortunately there is a deluge of examples where journalists have failed to do so.

One such instance is where a newspaper created the false impression that a city council had acted illegally regarding a "billing crisis" by not considering itself to be bound by its own by-laws. Talking about causing unnecessary harm…

One of accuracy's most deadly enemies is assumption. In the film *Silence of the Lambs* Jodie Foster's boss says to her: "If you assume, you are making an ass out of you and me" (ass-u-me).

I have had a case where a video of a celebrity was only partly seen by the journalist. The first part showed stuff that looked like cocaine. The article alleged that this celebrity was a drug addict and that she partook in a sex orgy.

Now, even if it was cocaine, how could the journalist have been sure of that? But, let's say for the sake of argument that it was cocaine, on what basis was the celebrity said to have been a drug "addict" (the film did not show that she used drugs, let alone being an addict); and even worse, the journalist had seen no evidence of any orgy whatsoever. When I asked the publication about this, it argued that the journalist "assumed" that there must have been an orgy after drugs have been taken — and that the celebrity was part of that scene. There was no proof; it was merely an assumption.

Accuracy and fairness go hand in hand — if a statement is inaccurate, and it unnecessarily harms someone, it is also bound to be unfair to that person. Therefore, "accurately" naturally leads to "fairly".

Fairly

"Fair" means "reasonable" and "balanced".

A newspaper once called a certain South African businessman a "tenderpreneur". This term (tender + entrepreneur) specifically refers to South African government officials and politicians who use their power and influence to secure government tenders and contracts. This businessman did get a government contract — but the mere fact that he has secured a contract did not make him a tenderpreneur. The newspaper failed to show that he also used his influence to obtain these contracts.

Surely, that was unfair (unreasonable) reporting, and the damage that it caused the subject was immeasurable.

Fairness also means "balanced". Here is a hypothetical example: A certain country has four political parties in Parliament — the ruling party has 60% support; the opposition has 30%; the third party amounts to 9%; and the smallest one's basis is 1%. Then there also are two tiny parties that are not represented in Parliament.

Clearly "fair" (balanced) reporting does not mean that a publication should give equal coverage to all six parties (depending on the nature of the issue, of course) – normally fairness dictates that the press should give *proportionate coverage* to the various parties.

> *2.2. News shall be presented in context and in a balanced manner, without any intentional or negligent departure from the facts whether by distortion, exaggeration or misrepresentation, material omissions, or summarisation.*

Context is as important as text. Here is an atrocious example: A journalist once reported that a certain city councilor had been involved in a financial scandal before linking it to allegations involving another incident. That piece of information was accurate (it was true that he had been involved in a scandal) – but the reporter neglected to add that there had been an enquiry into the scandal and that this specific councilor had been exonerated of all alleged wrong-doings. This context would have put the matter in a completely different light, but clearly in this case it did not suit the journalist – to the detriment of the (innocent and unfortunate) councilor. The journalist clearly did not allow facts to stand in the way of his story.

In another case, a journalist reported on medical parole that had been given to a controversial figure (under alleged controversial circumstances). He reported only one medical reason for the parole in a story that was highly critical of the matter. However, officials told the reporter that there were two other main reasons for this person's release. The journalist neglected to report these reasons, because clearly it did not suit his story.

The following example from the Bible also shows the importance of context (please note that I am not preaching!): There is a text in the Bible that says, "There is no God". So, if you cite those words you would be accurate. But that is misleading, as the preceding words put it into context. They namely say: "The fool says that..." (there is no God). This is a classic illustration of just how important context is.

Context requires balance (read: reasonable, fair reporting). The disturbing fact is that one can depart from the facts by distorting them, by exaggerating or misrepresenting them, by omitting and summarising material information – and by misrepresenting the context.

In my experience it is not always what journalists write that is unethical, but more often than not it is what they do not report that is problematical.

> *2.3. Only what may reasonably be true, having regard to the sources of the news, may be presented as fact, and such facts shall be published fairly with due regard to context and importance. Where a report is not based on facts or is founded on opinion, allegation, rumour or supposition, it shall be presented in such manner as to indicate this clearly.*

Journalists should not publish information from a source that cannot be reasonably true. Reporters should always discern the credibility of their sources and their information, and make proper decisions accordingly.

Secondly, never portray an opinion/allegation/rumour/supposition (yours, or that of somebody else) as fact. Journalists often start off by duly attributing the information, but then go ahead and present the source's opinion as fact. This happens in the blink of an eye, so take care! It must at all times be clear that opinion etc. is just that, and not fact.

Sub-editors can also easily make this mistake in either the editing process or in a headline. (Remember, sub-editors are also journalists.)

> *2.4. Where there is reason to doubt the accuracy of a report and it is practicable to verify the accuracy thereof, it shall be verified. Where it has not been practicable to verify the accuracy of a report, this shall be stated in such report.*

The Code demands that you should verify your information if you have reason to doubt the accuracy thereof. This means that you need not verify your information if you do not have reason to doubt that it is accurate.

For example, if a funeral is going to be held and you need to establish on what day and at what time it is going to commence, the vicar's word is enough for me. In that case, there is no need to verify the information. Or a sports team has won the national title – everybody knows that it is true, and you really do not have to phone the captain or the manager to verify that the team has really won. Conversely, if you have reason to doubt the accuracy of your information, you should try to verify it.

This clause does not state it explicitly, but the spirit of it is that journalists should verify their information *if that is likely to harm somebody*. The more important the information and the more likely that it can cause somebody harm, the greater the need for verification; and *vice versa*. If you were in the end unable to verify your information, you should state it in your story.

Please note that verification can only be achieved with *primary* and *independent* sources. Consider this:

Normally no publication is a *primary* source. The mere fact that information was published does not make it true. This means that if you use your archives, you may simply succeed in perpetrating a lie which, if the public starts to believe it, becomes "fact". One can only verify information from primary sources. Newspapers often provide me with published stories to try and "prove" that their stories were accurate. These are empty arguments, as they do not prove anything. In one such instance a prominent political leader was said to own a home worth R16 million. Eventually he lodged a complaint with my office, and the publication in question merely provided me with news reports that said the same.

However, the information turned out to be false – I contacted the relevant architects, who provided me with a certificate that stated that the total value of the property was R8.5 million. Clearly, the press all too easily merely repeat other reports – to such an extent that the R16 million eventually became "reality". In the meantime, nobody took the trouble to verify this "information" with a primary source – and a lie eventually became "fact" in the public's perception; and

Verification should be obtained from *independent* sources. For example, if you get data from someone, that person's spouse or child is not sufficiently independent to verify the information.

> *2.5. A publication shall seek the views of the subject of critical reportage in advance of publication; provided that this need not be done where the publication has reasonable grounds for believing that by doing so it would be prevented from publishing the report or where evidence might be destroyed or sources intimidated. Reasonable time should be afforded the subject for a response. If the publication is unable to obtain such comment, this shall be stated in the report.*

This is one of the most common mistakes that journalists seem to make all the time. It is a surprising fact that over 90% of all complaints lodged with me include the issue that "I was not asked for comment prior to publication" (regarding critical reportage).

This is astonishing, because surely it is one of the most fundamental maxims of journalism – listen to the other side, and report that. It is downright unfair to write about someone (who is likely to be harmed) without asking that person his/her opinion. How you would have felt if a publication writes something negative about you without giving you a right of reply?

However, this does not apply in all circumstances. Firstly, note the phrase "critical reportage". Again, the issue is about possible harm. If it is likely that your story can cause someone harm (rightly or wrongly), journalists are ethically bound to ask that person for comment.

This means that the less innocuous your story, the less there is a need to ask for comment. The general rule is that you should always ask for comment when there is any likelihood that the subject of your reportage can be harmed.

For example, if a journalist reports on a new appointment at the local school, it surely is not necessary to get comment (although you may ask for it, of course) – because your reportage is not "critical" (read: likely to cause harm).

Or when a soccer player is named Man of the Match you may report that he was awarded this honour without asking him for comment – as this reportage is not likely to cause him any harm. (Again, the journalist may ask this person for comment, but it is not unethical not to do so.)

But this clause also does not apply to all instances of critical reportage. For example, if you do court reporting you are not obliged to ask for comment – you are in fact not allowed to do so as the matter is *sub judice* and you may adversely affect court procedures if you do so. Once the other side has had a chance to testify in court that is the time when you report the other side.

Here are some examples of cases where journalists should have asked for comment, but didn't:

- One reporter's excuse was that a certain organistion always ignored her, so she decided it was not worth her while to try again. I ruled that it was her duty to try again – journalists should always try to solicit comment, even if circumstances are dire.

- One story implicated a former provincial premier of corruption on a massive scale. For some strange reason the publication never asked him for comment – as it should have as it had the potential to cause him huge unnecessary harm.

- A government department complained that a story falsely created the impression that the newspaper had interviewed its spokesperson. It then appeared that the publication quoted from a memorandum, falsely creating the impression that the journalist had interviewed this spokesperson.

- A Sunday weekly journalist started to work on a Wednesday on an important and sensitive story involving two of the most prominent politicians in South Africa. He contacted many people for comment – but only at the very last moment (on the Saturday afternoon, when the politician was playing golf) he asked the main subject of his reportage for comment. The fact that he asked him so late amounted, for all intents and purposes, to not asking him at all.

If these neglects to ask for comment were fair (read: reasonable, balanced), somebody needs to explain the term to me. So: Get comment from the person whom you are reporting on if your reportage is likely to harm that subject. Give that person enough time to comment meaningfully. If you cannot get comment, then state it in your story.

This clause also contains a safeguard that journalists need not get comment if the publication has reasonable grounds for believing that by doing so it would be prevented from publishing the report or where evidence might be destroyed or sources intimidated.

2.6. A publication shall make amends for publishing information or comment that is found to be inaccurate by printing, promptly and with appropriate prominence, a retraction, correction or explanation.

Sometimes, a complainant does not address the complaint directly to the Ombudsman's office, but rather confronts the publication itself. If the publication realises that it has made a mistake, either in its news columns or in its editorials, it should then rectify the matter immediately ("promptly").

It should also do it "with appropriate prominence". The problem, though, is that publications often obfuscate such corrections by placing a short sentence or two at the bottom of a page, obviously in an attempt to minimise their guilt. Clearly, this is not good enough.

When the Ombudsman's office directs a correction, we normally write the text ourselves, and we always state on what page it should be published and how prominent it should be presented.

Where there is no formal press regulation, such as in Mauritius, the onus is all the more on publications not only to publish retractions, corrections, explanations or apologies promptly, but also with appropriate prominence – which is only fair to the person or institution who has been harmed needlessly.

> *2.7. Reports, photographs or sketches relating to indecency or obscenity shall be presented with due sensitivity to the prevailing moral climate. A visual presentation of explicit sex shall not be published, unless public interest dictates otherwise.*

The term "prevailing moral climate" is a difficult one as morality changes all the time, albeit gradually. What was morally out of bounds some time ago may be quite acceptable at a later stage.

In multi-cultural societies the concept "moral climate" is even more complicated. For example, in parts of the black culture in South Africa witchcraft and sangomas are quite normal; in white culture these practices are unacceptable.

The press should be extremely sensitive to the morals and practices of different cultures and what is acceptable to some and not to others. The terms "indecency" and "obscenity" are equally nebulous.

But note what an American judge once said regarding pornography: "I cannot define it, but I know when I see it." Likewise, most people can identify indecency and obscenity when they see it, and are able to comprehend the prevailing moral climate (even in different cultures).

The Code asks journalists to act "sensitively" and to weigh up all matters relating to indecency, obscenity, and the prevailing moral climate.

These considerations are also important:

- The Code does not prohibit indecent and obscene reporting as such – it merely states that the publication of these matters should be presented "with due sensitivity" to the moral climate;

- The publication of explicit sex is not banned altogether – it is qualified by public interest; and

- The kind of publication that publishes such material is of critical importance. For example, one would not expect indecent or obscene pictures, and certainly not explicit sex pictures, in a family or religious magazine.

I once had a complaint about four pictures. The first three were of topless women, and the last one showed a naked couple hugging each other.

I dismissed this complaint on the following grounds:

- The pictures of topless women did not portray "explicit sex" – there is a vital difference between sex and nudity;

- The only question that remained was if these pictures were indecent or obscene;

- I then took into account the nature of the publication – would its readers have expected to see such pictures? In this instance, the answer was "yes". If these pictures were published in a newspaper where readers would not expect to see them, I would have found against the publication; and

- The fourth picture did indeed depict "explicit sex", but in this instance the man concerned was more than a public figure – he had heroic statues, and he was also commenting on sports events on TV. He was a role model, and I decided that the public had a right to know about his (extra-marital) behaviour.

You may have decided otherwise – as long as you have consciously put all the principles and consequences on the table. Media ethics is indeed not an exact science!

2.8. Journalists shall not plagiarise.

This is one of the worst faces of unethical journalism imaginable. Reporters work with words, and if they take over text from somebody else without acknowledging this fact, they are stealing from that journalist and are consequently betraying the very trade that they (should) hold so dearly.

Note that it is not prohibited to take over text from somebody else, but then you should limit it to the minimum and clearly state that you borrowed from that person.

The most common errors in this regard are twofold: Sometimes journalists simply cut and paste from the internet, and then put their name to it; or reporters merely publish press releases, again under their own names. I have seen examples of these practices.

To me, such journalists do not belong in the industry. They make their living by writing – and if they use somebody else's work under their own names, they are defying the very purpose of what they should be striving for.

3. Independence and conflicts of interest

3.1 The press shall not allow commercial, political, personal or other non-professional considerations to influence or slant reporting. Conflicts of interest must be avoided, as well as arrangements or practices that could lead audiences to doubt the press's independence and professionalism.

The preamble to the Code already mentioned this vital aspect – be, and stay, independent. By that we mean that journalists should never allow any influence to slant their reporting. If that happens, the publication would invariably lose its credibility.

"Commercial": All journalists are subject to this danger, but especially so financial reporters. For example, some journalists succumb to the temptation to write favourably about shares that they own in order to boost the value of these shares. There are many other such examples.

"Political": This problem is even more common. Each and every journalist has the right to hold political views and even to support a specific political party. As citizens they have the right to do so. However, they should not allow their political persuasions to slant their reporting. Surely, it is best not to be a member of that party.

"Personal": I have had examples of this. In one such a case, a journalist unfairly (because her facts were wrong) advocated a point of view because it would have been beneficial to her interests in a specific project. All of these amount to conflicts of interest.

But this article goes further: Not only should journalists consider their own positions, they should also contemplate what *impression* their actions may create. That is why the Code adds that "arrangements or practices that could lead audiences to doubt the press's independence and professionalism" should be avoided. Perceptions are realities in the eyes of the beholder. So: Even if your conscience is clear, you still need to consider the effect (consequences) of your actions.

For example: My office used to be adjacent to that of the South African Editors' Forum (Sanef). Remember, members of Sanef are one party to a complaint – the complainant is the other party. The Ombudsman is a referee – in the middle, not taking sides, but I adjudicate on merit.

Now, as Ombudsman I was never influenced by the fact that Sanef was just next door. We could even have shared the same office as far as I was concerned. It did not matter to me where I work, as

I was convinced that nothing from outside would influence my decisions.

However, certain circles in public had their doubts as to my office's independence (because of Sanef's close proximity to the Ombudsman's office). So, even though it did not influence my rulings in the least, we decided to move to a different premise – to avoid the perception that our independence and professionalism could be compromised.

> *3.2 Journalists shall not accept a bribe, gift or any other benefit where this is intended or likely to influence coverage.*

In South Africa, we have had several instances of alleged political interference with reporting. For example, it was said that a certain politician had paid a journalist to write favourably about him. If that was true, the money certainly influenced his reporting. This is serious stuff.

But let's look at this clause more closely. It does not say that journalists may never accept anything – it merely states that reporters should not accept gifts etc. *"where this is intended or likely to influence coverage"*.

If, for example, a political party holds a press conference and it provides you with some writing material, surely that is not likely to influence your reporting. However, for the sake of argument, if the pen that that party provides you with is made from gold, that may be likely to influence some reporters.

Regarding the use of the word "intended". Sometimes it is clear that the gift is intended to influence your reporting (if the example mentioned above turns out to be accurate, then it is as clear as daylight that the politician intended to influence reporting).

However, most givers would deny any such intentions. "Just come with us to a game resort for the weekend – no strings attached." In many of these cases the journalist would not be sure if there is any intention involved. The question then should always be: "But why this invitation?"

That is why the next clause is so important: "...or likely to (influence coverage)". Again, this is a judgment call. The point is to always be on the alert – never accept anything that may influence your reporting or that may create the impression that it is likely to happen. Again: Remember that perceptions are realities. Be careful not to be party to a situation that may create the wrong impressions that may lead to wrong perceptions, even though you may be convinced that you would not be influenced by a gift.

That is why I, as Ombudsman, shall never accept an invitation from a publication to (say) attend a sports occasion with its journalists.

> *3.3 The press shall indicate clearly when an outside organisation has contributed to the cost of newsgathering.*

This article does not prohibit the practice of outside organisations paying journalists to cover an event. It does, though, make it clear that in such instances the reporter should indicate this. The reason is obvious – if an outside organization has contributed to the cost of newsgathering at least that may create a perception that the journalist may be influenced to write favourably about the sponsors. The public needs to know this, which would place it in a position to decide for itself if the reporting was slanted or not.

Motoring journalists travel abroad on a regular basis and in many instances their publications do not pay for it. So be it – as long as it is made clear that an outside organization has done the honours.

There also is nothing wrong when (say) a foreign government invites you to its country to cover its elections. This happened to me once, when the German government invited me for that very reason – but then, the public had a right to know that my publication did not cover the costs.

So state it.

3.4 Editorial material shall be kept clearly distinct from advertising.

Under "advertising" I mean both advertisements and advertorials.

This article, and the reason for it, should be read in the context of that which precedes it (read: independence). Advertisements and advertorials should be "kept clearly distinct" from editorial material because if not, the publication's very independence is at stake.

4. Dignity, Reputation and Privacy

4.1. The press shall exercise care and consideration in matters involving the private lives and concerns of individuals. The right to privacy may be overridden by a legitimate public interest.

Privacy does not mean the same thing to everybody; we need to distinguish between public officials, public figures (celebrities), and ordinary citizens.

Public officials have the least right to privacy because they are getting paid with taxpayers' money – which means that they are accountable to the public, which in turn means that it is the duty of the press to hold these people accountable. Public officials have no ground to complain if the press reveals their private matters when these matters have a bearing on their public duty.

To a lesser extent, but still so, public figures should also be held accountable for their actions. They are role models, especially for the youth, and the press therefore has the right to report on their private lives if that impacts on their roles in society.

Private citizens have the most right to privacy. For example, if your gardener has an extra-marital affair, publications should (normally) ignore it as it is of little or no significance to the public. (However, if the president has such an affair, or some celebrity, that would probably be news.)

The Code states that the press should exercise "care and consideration" in matters involving privacy and that this right "may be overridden by a legitimate public interest".

So:

- The press should not treat people's privacy lightly – journalists should be careful and consider this issue carefully; and

- In each and every case, the journalist's question should be: "If I am going to invade somebody's privacy, is it really in the public interest to do so?"

This begs the question when a person is in private.

I have had complaints from angry citizens that the press has photographed their houses without their consent. I have consistently dismissed these complaints, as their houses were in public. It would have been a different matter, though, if a journalist would enter the premises without permission, or "steal" pictures through windows (unless a public interest would allow the photographer to do so, of course).

Also, a person once said that a journalist took a picture of her while she was shopping and complained that that had invaded her privacy. She had no leg to stand on – the moment she left her home, she gave up her privacy.

Once, a famous sportsman was kissing a woman in a park – while he was married to another woman. The press reported this matter, not only because he was a celebrity, but also because the park was a public place.

The definition of privacy is complicated, and it is a rather modern and mostly Western concept. But let's simplify it: One is private in one's home, or in a private place that is in public (like a bathroom).

One cannot be private in public.

> *4.2. The press shall exercise care and consideration in matters involving dignity and reputation. The dignity or reputation of an individual should only be overridden in the following circumstances:*
>
> > *4.2.1. The facts reported are true or substantially true;*

4.2.2. The article amounts to fair comment based on facts that are adequately referred to and that are true or substantially true;

4.2.3. The report amounts to a fair and accurate report of court proceedings, Parliamentary proceedings or the proceedings of any quasi-judicial tribunal or forum; or

4.2.4. It was reasonable for the article to be published because it was prepared in accordance with acceptable principles of journalistic conduct and in the public interest.

There are many definitions of dignity, but they all have in common the quality or state of being worth of esteem and respect. The operative word here is "worth".

This clause has therefore to do with defamation, which I define as any intentional false communication that harms a person's reputation; decreases the respect, regard, or confidence in which a person is held; or induces disparaging, hostile, or disagreeable opinions or feelings against a person. In short, defamation is the malicious, unfair, significant lowering of one's public image (which was worthy of dignity and reputation).

Reputation can be defined as the general esteem in which a person is held by the public. Again, the Code does not forbid all instances of the lowering of a person's dignity and reputation. It depends if it is true or not. You cannot defame somebody with the truth. If it is true that the mayor stole money, you may state it without fear of defaming him or her.

However, in South African law something more is needed: The lowering of somebody's dignity and reputation must *also* be in the public interest.

But there is more – when you lower somebody's public image, you then have to be able to *prove* that your allegations are true. You cannot simply publish at a whim. This proof may not always be easy to achieve. So, when you are not sure of your facts, rather do not publish if your story is likely to significantly lower someone's reputation. If you are sure, nothing should stop you to publish (if it is true and dictated by public interest).

The same goes for an opinion article – the significant lowering of someone's reputation should be based on facts (see the section below that deals with "Comment").

Journalists may also report court, parliamentary, or any quasi-judicial tribunal's proceedings that significantly lower someone's reputation without fear of defamation, provided that they do so accurately and fairly.

But in normal circumstances: If a source makes a defamatory statement about a person and you report this statement, you also commit defamation. Remember that the repetition of defamation is also defamation. It is no excuse to say that you have not made the allegation, and that you have merely reported what the source said. I have encountered this lame excuse numerous times.

Note that you cannot defame a dead person. Defamation laws are designed to protect peoples' interests – and a dead person does not have any interests anymore.

In this one instance, two male farm workers were accused of killing a famous right-wing leader (also male). However, some stories reported that the workers had sex with him before murdering him. That reporting could not have defamed the murdered man, as he was dead; however, it could have defamed the farm workers (if the rumours were not true).

Note the four exceptions to this clause, and the word "or" at the end of the third. This implies that only one of these exceptions is necessary to satisfy the Code's demands.

> *4.3. The identity of rape victims and victims of sexual violence shall not be published without the consent of the victim or in the case of children, without the consent of their legal guardians and it is in the best interest of the child.*

A journalist may not publish the identity of a rape victim and victims of sexual violence (people who are over 18 years old) if these victims do not consent. It follows that you may disclose their identities if they do consent. It is as simple as that. The important consideration is that this decision is up to the victim – not up to the journalist. A reporter does not have the right to decide for adults what is good for them.

The matter is different when it comes to children. The Code firstly says that the revealing of a child's identity is up to its legal guardian.

But what if these guardians are not representing the best interests of a child? They may have ulterior motives, or (for argument's sake) may even be drunk at the time.

This is where the journalist comes in. It is namely not enough to obtain the consent of the guardians – *the reporter should also be convinced that it is in the best interest of the child to do so*. This is an extremely sensitive issue, and the decision to reveal a child's identity should be taken with the utmost care. The responsibility on the journalist's shoulders is enormous.

Although the Code does not touch on the say that a child may have in such a situation, the journalist should be flexible and take the age of the child into consideration. Let's go to extremes: If a baby of one month old is raped, clearly that child cannot make any contribution. But let's say that the child is about to become 18 (an adult) in a few days' time – in that case, I would also ask that person for his or her permission.

The Code should be applied with discretion. Never only rely on the letter only; always take into account the spirit of the Code as well.

> *4.4. The HIV/AIDS status of people should not be disclosed without their consent, or in the case of children, without the consent of their legal guardians, and only if it is in the public interest and it is in the best interest of the child.*

HIV/AIDS is singled out above those of (for example) cancer, malaria and TB, as it carries a stigma to it, unlike most other diseases.

The same argument regarding children, as discussed immediately above, applies here – with the addition that public interest is also a condition for revealing the information.

5. Discrimination and Hate Speech

5.1. Except where it is strictly relevant to the matter reported and it is in the public interest to do so, the press shall avoid discriminatory or denigratory references to people's race, gender, sex, pregnancy, marital status, ethnic or social origin, colour, sexual orientation, age, disability, religion, conscience, belief, culture, language and birth or other status, nor shall it refer to people's status in a prejudicial or pejorative context.

Let's take a look at what this clause says and then at what it does not say. It namely urges the press to avoid "discriminatory" and "denigratory" references to people's race, etc. It adds that it shall not refer to people's status in a "prejudicial" or "pejorative" context.

In practice, this means that all unnecessary and negative references mentioned in the article should be avoided. If, for example, a gay person was run over by a car, it is not necessary to state that person's sexual orientation (unless, of course, it is relevant to the matter).

What it does not say, is that you may not refer to a person's status at all. However, it should under all circumstances be "strictly relevant" to the matter reported on and in the public interest to do so. For example, if a white male in his fourties has raped women and the Police are on his trail, it would for obvious reasons be in the public interest for the press to mention his colour, sex and age.

Again, more is at stake here than meets the eye. This has to do with stereotyping. "Stereotyping" is derived from the Greek words "stereos" (firm, solid) and "typos" (impression). The term therefore means "solid impression".

The University of Colorado correctly describes stereotyping as "generalizations, or assumptions, that people make about the characteristics of all members of a group, based on an image (often wrong) about what people in that group are like".[1] The University explains further:

> "For example, one study of stereotypes revealed that Americans are generally considered to be friendly, generous, and tolerant, but also arrogant, impatient, and domineering. Asians, on the other hand, were expected to be shrewd and alert, but reserved. Clearly, not all Americans are friendly and generous; and not all Asians are shrewd. If you assume you know what a person is like, and don't look at each person as an individual, you are likely to make errors in your estimates of a person's character.

> "In conflicts, people tend to develop overly-negative images of the other side. The opponent is expected to be aggressive, self-serving, and deceitful, for example, while people view themselves in completely positive ways. These stereotypes tend to be self-perpetuating. If one side assumes the other side is deceitful and aggressive, they will tend to respond in a similar way. The opponent will then develop a similar image of the first party, and the negative stereotypes will be confirmed. They may grow worse, as communication is shut down and escalation heightens emotions and tension."

Each and every society has its own stereotypes. The point here is that the press should be careful not to perpetuate these stereotypes. The press needs to treat each person and situation on merit.

> *5.2. The press has the right and indeed the duty to report and comment on all matters of legitimate public interest. This right and duty must, however, be balanced against the obligation not to publish material that amounts to:*

> *5.2.1. Propaganda for war;*

> *5.2.2. Incitement of imminent violence; or*

---

1 http://www.colorado.edu/conflict/peace/problem/stereoty.htm

5.2.3. Advocacy of hatred that is based on race, ethnicity, gender or religion, and that constitutes incitement to cause harm.

It is important to note that the Code does not only say that the press has the "right" to report and comment on all matters of legitimate public interest – it is indeed its "duty" to do so.

The rest of this clause has already been dealt with under the preamble. The point is that even the right to freedom of speech has boundaries and is not absolute, as the duty to report and comment has to be "balanced" against the obligation not to commit hate speech.

Yet again: Even the freedom of expression is not absolute.

6. Advocacy

A publication is justified in strongly advocating its own views on controversial topics provided that it treats its readers fairly by:

6.1. Making fact and opinion clearly distinguishable;

6.2. Not misrepresenting or suppressing relevant facts; and

6.3. Not distorting the facts.

This clause allows the press to (strongly) advocate its views on any important matter (politics, economy, social issues, ecology, whatever).

It should be noted that this does not apply to news reports – it only allows a publication to express its views in an editorial or opinion column.

In doing so, fact and opinion should be clearly distinguishable, the publication should clarify that it is its views (opinion, not fact), and ensure that it did not ignore or distort relevant facts. I have not received a single complaint regarding this clause.

I need to make two general remarks here:

- The comment that is mentioned here, is strictly limited to editorial articles and opinion pieces – it most certainly does not extend to news reporting;

- It is a telling fact that the word "fairly" or "fair" appears in each of the sub-divisions under this heading. If that does not say something about the quality of comment that the Code requires of the press when commenting on affairs of public interest, nothing will; and

- The words "honestly", "truly stated" and "honest" also appear in all three sub-divisions. This is as important. Nothing is worse than a dishonest opinion.

7. Comment

7.1. The press shall be entitled to comment upon or criticise any actions or events of public interest provided such comments or criticisms are fairly and honestly made.

This clause gives the press the much-needed freedom to comment on or criticize any matter of public interest that it sees fit. It is necessary for the sake of freedom of speech and for the robustness of the debate.

I shall discuss the "fairly" and "honestly" part under Art. 7.3.

7.2. Comment by the press shall be presented in such manner that it appears clearly that it is comment, and shall be made on facts truly stated or fairly indicated and referred to.

Always indicate an opinion article as such. I have not encountered any problem with this section of the Code, as (in my experience) publications without exception consistently indicate clearly when it is commenting on a matter. This should be the case. Always.

Again, the words "truly stated" and "fairly indicated and referred to" are used.

7.3. Comment by the press shall be an honest expression of opinion, without malice or dishonest motives, and shall take fair account of all available facts which are material to the matter commented upon.

The SA Constitutional Court has ruled in April 2011 (Robert McBride vs. National Media) as follows: "Criticism is protected even if extreme, unjust, unbalanced, exaggerated and prejudiced, as long as it expresses an honestly held opinion, without malice, on a matter of public interest on facts that are true."

Note the words "honestly held opinion", "malice" and "dishonest motives" ("fairness" finds a snug place in the concept "malice") in the verdict; also the mutual use of the word "malice". Clearly, the Press Code shares the court's conviction.

Here are some examples of transgressions that I have encountered that did not take "fair account of all available facts which are material to the matter commented upon":

- A prominent politician once said at a conference in Johannesburg that the media are "like a pack of dogs". One newspaper reported this correctly, but the editor of the same publication then accused this politician of stating that he said that the media *are* dogs. To some this may seem like splitting hairs, but it certainly is not. There is a world of difference between these two statements – the first one points to a verb (the media *act* like dogs); the second one to a noun (the media *are* dogs). Without stereotyping the matter, one must remember that in black culture dogs are often seen as one of the lowest forms of life. I directed the newspaper to apologise for this mistake to minimise the unnecessary harm that if caused this politician.

- When a prominent right-wing (white) leader (of an all-white organization) was murdered (I have already referred to this case, but in a different context), a journalist wrote an opinion piece after having attended his funeral. This columnist accused the murdered man's organization of having killed a (black) mayor. The reporter was entitled to his opinion, but he did not take all available facts into account. In this instance, a court had already convicted a black man (who could not have belonged to the all-white organization) for the murder of the mayor. If the columnist had stated that he knew about the court case but disagreed with the outcome, that would have been in order – because then he would have taken this vital piece of available fact into account (with which he did not have to agree with). However, he neglected to do this.

• A hospital complained that an opinion piece unfairly said that the Department of Health had appointed "fake" medical practitioners, nurses and doctors. The hospital justifiably argued that its staff had been all registered with the Health Professional Council of South Africa and that they therefore could not have been "fake". Again, the journalist did not take fair account of all available facts.

Always take account of all relevant facts. After that, you can express your opinion (within the boundaries of hate speech, defamation and malice, of course). I define "malice" as the desire to inflict injury, harm, or suffering on another, either because of a hostile impulse or out of deep-seated meanness.[2]

Cartoons may be seen as comment and therefore it also falls under this section. I regard cartoons as satire and believe that cartoonists enjoy a huge amount of freedom to express their views (also always within boundaries, of course).

Here are some examples that I have encountered:

A municipality complained that the cartoonist "intended to cause maximum harm to the image of the Nelson Mandela Bay Municipality (in Port Elizabeth) and its employees". It described the cartoon as a deliberate attack on the intellectual capacity of its

2 http://dictionary.reference.com/browse/malice

administration, saying that it had made "a political statement" and that it was racist.

The story was about a farmer who used a horse to plough his land because of the high cost of petrol. The cartoon consisted of a four-panel piece that was about the use of horses for transport. The top two panels of the cartoon said: "If we went back to horse power, things would change for the better..." The third panel showed people scattering as a horse and rider caused mayhem. The fourth one portrayed a horse pushing the cart – labelled "municipality" – and carrying four people. The words above the third and fourth panels were: "or would they?"

Unlike the complainant, I found the criticism in this instance to be mild and certainly not malicious, as I did not believe that there was a hostile or mean desire on the cartoonist's part to inflict injury, harm, or suffering on the municipality. It was rather a legitimate expression of an honest opinion (held by many other people). The cartoonist may have been wrong, for all I care – but still he had a right to voice his opinion (within the guidelines of the relevant articles in the Code).

In a very real sense, both the Press Code and the country's Constitution give people the right to be wrong.

There are quite a few famous examples of cartoons depicting the Muslim prophet Muhammad. I am always wary of any such cartoons (even if they are not critical of the prophet or the Islam religion), as the Muslim community worldwide believes that any picture or sketch Muhammad amounts to blasphemy.

The cartoonist may not share this belief – but, knowing full well that it offends the Muslim community, and contemplating the consequences that any such cartoon may have, the newspaper should be careful and tread lightly.

The same sensitivity should be exercised with regard to other religions. Each situation should be considered on its own merits.

8. Children

The Bill of Rights (Section 28.2) in the South African Constitution states: "A child's best interests are of paramount importance in every matter concerning the child."

This clause cites a part of South Africa's Constitution. Clearly, both the Constitution and the Press Council take the "best interests" of a child seriously – which is good and appropriate.

Note the careful way in which this sentence is constructed:

- It does not mention "children" (plural, which may have amounted to a generalisation), but it is about a specific child (singular) – each and every child is an individual, unique, precious and important, and s/he should be treated as such;

- It is not only about a child's interests, it is about his/her "best" interests;

- Most importantly, the specification that a child's best interests are of "paramount importance" should not be taken lightly – this is the first and only time that the Code qualifies a matter in such radical terms; and

- As if that is not enough, the clause adds that this importance is relevant in "every" matter that concerns a "child" (singular, again). There are no exceptions, nor should there be.

If this sentence does not alert the press to be extremely careful when reporting about a child, nothing will.

8.1. The press shall therefore exercise exceptional care and consideration when reporting about children under the age of 18. If there is any chance that coverage might cause harm of any kind to a child, he or she shall not be interviewed, photographed or identified unless a custodial parent or similarly responsible adult consents, or a public interest is evident.

This clause was also carefully construed, and it should be read as meticulously as it was worded. The fourth word "therefore" is operative here as it links the powerful preceding sentence with the one under discussion. This is quite significant.

But there is more. In some instances the Code asks journalists to take "care and consideration". In this instance it notably adds the word "exceptional" to the "care and consideration", which (again) implies that the press should take this clause extremely seriously.

This is the principle: If there is *any chance* that coverage might cause a child harm of any kind, s/he should not be interviewed, photographed or identified unless a custodial parent consents or a public interest is evident. In this case, there are no exceptions. There should be none.

These are the implications:

- When there is no likelihood that a child can be harmed by a story or a picture, there is nothing wrong with reporting that matter. For example, two schools compete in their yearly soccer clash. The journalist takes pictures of children on the pavilion, cheering their teams on. You don't need anybody's permission to publish those pictures, as it is not likely that that would harm any child. The same does not go for (for example) a child in an orphanage home. Such a picture has the potential to be harmful to the child – so even if your intentions are good, you will do well to re-consider and re-re-consider before you decide to publish.

- It is up to the journalist/publication to decide if a certain matter regarding a child is in the public interest. Just imagine what responsibility this entails.

8.2. Child pornography shall not be published.

Child Pornography is defined in the Film and Publications Act as: Any image or any description of a person, real or simulated, who is or who is depicted or described as being, under the age of 18 years, engaged in sexual conduct; participating in or assisting another person to participate in sexual conduct; or showing or describing the body or parts of the body of the person in a manner or parts of the body of the person in a manner or circumstance which, in context, amounts to sexual exploitation.

There is no excuse for publishing child pornography. That is the long and the short of it. Child pornography is prohibited, and as far as I am concerned it will (and should) be banned forever.

8.3. The press shall not identify children who have been victims of abuse, exploitation, or who have been charged with or convicted of a crime, unless a public interest is evident and it is in the best interests of the child.

Note the two qualifications here: A child victim or a convicted or charged child may only be identified if it is in the public's interest *and* if it is in that child's best interests. The word "and" implies that *both* conditions should be met. This is of paramount importance, as the onus is once again placed on the journalist to make a responsible decision in this regard.

9. Violence

Due care and responsibility shall be exercised by the press with regard to the presentation of brutality, violence and suffering.

We live in a brutal, violent world that is used to suffering, and the public has a right to know about it. However, there is no need to over-kill. Anything does not go. This clause asks for "care and responsibility" and refers to both text and pictures.

Firstly, text: Let me use an extreme example to try and make a point. Let me return to the mayor who was killed after his throat was slit. There is no need to report just how long and deep the cut was. Just think about the unnecessary pain and suffering that that would cause his loved ones.

The danger is greater when it comes to pictures. I have seen some atrocious examples of photographs that were really out of bounds.

Here are the principles that you can use when deciding if and how to publish such pictures:

- It has to be in the public interest;

- In the case of dead or heavily injured people, you may avoid causing unnecessary harm by considering to:

  - not identify the person (blocking out the person's face and other vital parts of the body – and doing so adequately);

  - not publish gross details of wounds;

  - use pictures in black and white;

  - use small pictures;

  - use pictures inside and not on the front page; and

  - warn sensitive readers on the front page.

Let me dwell on these issues for a while. The more a matter is in the public interest, the greater your freedom will be. For example, in 1966 South Africa's Prime Minister was stabbed to death in Parliament. Just about every newspaper in the country published his bloody face in colour on their front pages. The public interest was so overriding that this was deemed to be acceptable.

However, this would not have been the case when a largely unknown person was murdered – unless, of course, the case itself was in the overwhelming public interest.

I once had a complaint about a person who had died in a motor accident. Only the hand was visible – yet the family still complained. I dismissed it because the body had not been identified, nor did it reveal the extent of his injuries. I need to add, though, that I had sympathy with the family.

Sometimes publications are often not careful enough. In one such instance, a child took his own life by hanging himself to a tree (on school grounds). The newspaper published this picture, and only blocked out his eyes – but that was not enough as his parents and friends could still identify him. Think of the pain that this picture unnecessarily has caused them.

Some journalists argue that a warning of the front page is counter-productive as it would only serve to induce people to look at it. That may be true, but then that is their choice. By warning the public you have done your ethical duty.

Hereunder are three pictures that have to do with violence.

The first picture is about violence that broke out at a mine in South Africa. The police shot and killed tens of miners and wounded scores more. Naturally, it was big news at the time. The people in the picture were all dead.

The newspaper was justified in publishing this picture as:

- it was in the overwhelming public interest;

- none of the deceased could have been identified, as their faces were all turned away (with the possible exception of one); and

- no gruesome wounds were visible.

The same newspaper declined to use the second and third pictures (taken in the midst of the present Syrian crisis – all the people in these pictures were dead), as they were too gruesome and the deceased could have been identified.

10. Headlines, Posters, Pictures and Captions

10.1. Headlines and captions to pictures shall give a reasonable reflection of the contents of the report or picture in question.

If a story is well-written, the gist of the article is in the intro – from where the headline then usually follows. This ensures that the headline gives a reasonable reflection of the content of the report. If the story is badly written, it makes life difficult for sub-editors.

The most common mistake here is that headlines often portray an allegation as fact – even after the story has quite correctly presented an allegation as an allegation, and attributed it to a source. However, in writing the headline some thoughtless journalists often neglect to use inverted commas, or to attribute the statement.

For example: A story quotes sources who alleged that this public official (Mr X) "was" corrupt. The headline should read: *Mr X 'corrupt'*, or: *Mr X corrupt, sources say*. These are not statements of fact, as they show that they are people's opinion. It should not read *Mr X is corrupt*.

Also, note that when a story is inaccurate and this reflects in a headline or a caption, that headline or caption will also be wrong and therefore will also be in breach of the Code.

In one case, a story alleged that a prominent politician was lying about a certain matter (singular, one alleged lie). However, the headline stated: "Lies, lies and more lies". This was plural as well as a statement of fact, while the story referred only to *one, alleged* lie (the text quite correctly stated that as an allegation and not as fact).

Sub-editors should also be careful. As I have already said, they are also journalists who should accordingly adhere to the Code.

> *10.2. Posters shall not mislead the public and shall give a reasonable reflection of the contents of the reports in question.*

I once had a complaint from a provincial premier about a poster that stated it as fact that she had wasted millions of rands. However, the story attributed this allegation to a source – who was later found to be wrong. Talking about causing unnecessary harm... The publication had to apologise to her on the front page, above the fold, with the word "apology" and her name in the headline.

In another instance, a poster claimed that the wife of a prominent politician was guilty of drug smuggling. The fact that she was later convicted of this felony, still did not justify the publication to state it as fact at that stage – the court case had not even begun yet.

> *10.3. Pictures shall not misrepresent or mislead nor be manipulated to do so.*

This clause is concerned with both the cropping and manipulation of pictures.

Once, five colleagues were socialising in a bar after work. The story was about an alleged extra-marital relationship between two of them. The publication then "cleverly" (maliciously?) cropped the picture to make it seem as if the "couple" were on their own – which was not true. They were merely sitting next to each other, together with three other colleagues (who were cropped out of the picture).

There also is the world-famous example of picture manipulation when former Pres Nelson Mandela let loose two white doves after he had been released from jail. These doves were too far away from Mandela's hands to be used in the picture, so the publication manipulated it in order to fit.

This was an "innocent" manipulation, because it did not alter the meaning of what had happened. Yet, the publication should have mentioned that it doctored the picture. Very few journalistic practices erode the credibility of a newspaper more than this issue – the public invariably asks what else it cannot believe.

If, for practical reasons, a picture has to be manipulated, it should not change its meaning and the publication should inform the public about it.

11. Confidential and anonymous sources

11.1. The press has an obligation to protect confidential sources of information.

It is an extremely serious matter to give your word not to reveal the identity of your sources – Section 205 of the South African Criminal Procedures Act stipulates that the state may force a journalist to reveal her or his sources, or else s/he may go to jail. Therefore, journalists should carefully consider their decisions to keep their sources confidential. This is the principle: Once you have given your word not to reveal the source's identity, you should stick to it – and if you do, it may have dire consequences.

However, if you later discover that your source has (purposefully) misled you, you cannot be blamed for revealing that source's identity.

11.2. The press shall avoid the use of anonymous sources unless there is no other way to deal with a story. Care should be taken to corroborate the information.

In South Africa, the use of anonymous sources has become a major problem of late. The reason for this is that most government officials are scared to speak out, so some of them become whistle-blowers – but anonymous ones, at that. This is forcing the press to make use of these people, which is not a healthy situation at all.

The main reason for this clause is because unnamed people can say whatever they like, without having to be accountable – and the real problem is that they may have ulterior motives. I have indeed seen many times how anonymous sources had deliberately misled journalists in order to enhance their own agendas.

Politicians are the most dangerous in this regard. Some of them will go to extreme lengths to discredit their opponents. In one such instance a political party "analysed" a certain report. The newspaper then took the information contained in this "analysis" as gospel and published it as such. In the meantime, the analysis (purposefully?) misread and misinterpreted the report – with the result that the public was misled as well.

In another tragic case, a journalist reported that a certain prominent person in South Africa was not making himself available for election as deputy president of the ruling party. The senior political editor's information was the opposite, so she tried to stop the publication of that story. The reporter allegedly told her that she should trust him, as he trusted his (anonymous) sources. His story turned out to be false – and the political editor resigned as a result of that. I commend her for that, as I would have done the same. One can only speculate as to the motives of the sources that planted the incorrect information.

One more example: A school principal was suspended by the Department of Education, but at that stage it did not communicate any clear reason for its actions. Eight stories in other publications reported this matter, and all of them stated that the reason for his suspension was unclear.

However, one newspaper quoted a single, anonymous source saying that the reason was theft.

This turned out to be false, and the newspaper stated in a follow-up story that the source had spread malicious gossip. Yet, the journalist allowed herself to be misled by this source, and ended up causing the principal some huge, unnecessary harm.

Therefore, always:

- handle anonymous sources with the utmost of care – they may be very dangerous;

- try to convince your sources to go on record – you may only proceed if they are not willing to do that, provided that you cannot get the same information elsewhere, and the information is in the public interest; and

- corroborate their allegations – if you cannot do that, you should either not publish at all, or at the very least state that you were not able to corroborate the information. In that case, never state any allegation as fact.

11.3. The press shall not publish information that constitutes a breach of confidence, unless a legitimate public interest dictates otherwise.

Under normal circumstances, journalists should at all costs protect their sources and not publish information that breaches confidence. However, circumstances alter cases. For example, if a source tells you off the record that Parliament is going to be blown up, I submit that this information should be published in the public interest.

In this (extreme) case, consequences weigh much more than principles and certainly, public interest would override your pledge not to tell.

12. Payment for Articles

The press shall avoid shady journalism in which informants are paid to induce them to give the information, particularly when they are criminals – except where the material concerned ought to be published in the public interest and the payment is necessary for this to be done.

The practice of paying for information should be avoided because it:

- immediately puts the credibility of the information in doubt – will such a source tell you the truth, or instead what you want to hear?; and

- changes the relationship between the journalist and the source – the latter becomes a business partner, which may compromise your independence.

However, if the information is in the public interest and a journalist cannot obtain it otherwise, the Code does allow you to pay for information.

THE GIST OF THE CODE

Johan Retief

What follows, is a paraphrase and a summary of the Press Code and my comments on it, in an attempt to make it easier to digest. I recommend that news houses print both the Code and this summary and put it up where all journalists can see them.

Ethical journalism starts and ends by striving for truth, by avoiding unnecessary harm, and by not allowing outside influences to slant your reporting. If you stick to these ideals, you should be able to avoid acting unethically – and thereby serving society (which is what journalism is all about). Remember that your work should at all times be guided by public interest (information of legitimate interest or importance to citizens). Always show a special concern for children and other vulnerable groups, giving voice to the voiceless. Your freedom of expression, which you should defend at all costs, is not absolute as it does not include hate speech.

In order to reach these goals, the following matters should be pursued:

- Obtain your news legally, honestly and fairly, and identify yourself as a journalist, unless public interest dictates otherwise and there is no other way for you to obtain the information that you need.

- Report this news truthfully, accurately and fairly.

- Present your news in context and in a balanced manner – without distortion, exaggeration, misrepresentation, material

111

omissions or summarisation. Remember: context is as important as text.

- Do not portray an opinion (yours, or that of other people) as fact. Discern your information to establish whether it may reasonably be true.

- Verify your information with an independent source if you have reason to doubt the accuracy thereof. The more important the information, the greater the need for verification. If you cannot verify it, then state it in your story.

- Get comment from the person whom you are reporting about if your reporting is likely to cause harm. Give that subject enough time to comment meaningfully, depending on the nature of your enquiry. If you cannot get comment, then state it in your story.

- If you discover that you have made a mistake, then correct it promptly and with the necessary prominence.

- Be sensitive regarding matters of indecency and obscenity, and take cognizance of the prevailing moral climate. Do not publish explicit sex, unless public interest dictates otherwise.

- Don't plagiarise.

- Be, and stay, independent – don't allow anything to influence or slant your reporting.

- Indicate when an outside organization has contributed to the cost of newsgathering, and keep editorial material distinct from advertising.

- Respect people's privacy, dignity and reputation. This may be overridden only by a legitimate public interest.

- Do not identify rape victims, victims of sexual violence and the HIV/AIDS status of people without the necessary consent; also consider the best interests of children as well as the public interest.

- Avoid discriminatory or denigratory references to people's race, colour, ethnicity, religion, gender, sexual orientation or preference, physical or mental disability or illness, age, or other status, except where it is relevant to the matter reported. Don't even refer to it, unless it is relevant.

- You may report and comment on all matters of public interest, but avoid hate speech – your freedom of expression is not absolute.

- You may advocate your own views in opinion articles (not in news reports), provided that you treat your readers fairly by clearly distinguishing between fact and opinion, by not misrepresenting or suppressing relevant facts, and by not distorting them.

- Comment and criticism is allowed in opinion articles (not in news stories), provided that it is fairly and honestly made, presented in such a way that it is clear that it is comment, made on facts truly stated, an honest expression without malice or dishonest motives, and takes fair account of all available material facts.

- Be extremely careful when reporting on children (people under the age of 18). This is the principle: If there is any chance that coverage might cause a child harm of any kind, s/he should not be interviewed, photographed or identified unless a custodial parent consents or a public interest is evident. Child pornography is not allowed. Do not identify children who have been victims of abuse or exploitation, or who have been charged with or convicted of a crime, unless public interest dictates otherwise or it is in the child's best interests.

- Exercise due care and responsibility with regard to the presentation of brutality, violence and atrocities.

- Do not manipulate or crop pictures to misrepresent or mislead the public. Where it is necessary to manipulate a picture, then state it clearly. Ensure that headlines, captions and posters reasonably reflect the content of the story.

- Avoid the use of anonymous sources if at all possible. If you cannot get your information in any other way, take care to corroborate this information. If you do make use of an anonymous source, you are under an obligation to protect that source and not breach his/her confidence.

- Do not pay a source to get information, unless it is in the public interest and there is no other way to obtain the facts.

In conclusion: Adopt a Press Code, know it and live it.

Practicalities from the Ombusdman's Office

Tools of the trade

Here are some practical pointers that I make use of in my findings. You will notice that I am going to draw on most or all of what I have argued above.

The following tools should help journalists to make good ethical decisions:

Use a Press Code: A Press Code is an ethical compass without which journalists are all at sea when it comes to making difficult decisions for the right reasons. A Code contains the principles that journalists need to consider.

Principles, consequences, golden mean: When journalists are confronted with ethical choices, they should *every time* ask themselves what principles are at stake, and what possible consequences can come from publishing or from not publishing. Consider if there are tension between principles, between consequences, and between the two of these. If so, find a reasonable golden mean.

Strive for truth, minimise harm, stay independent: These are basic principles that are mentioned in every good media ethical handbook worldwide – and it also has everything to do with consequences. This is all-important as they are at the heart of the South African Press Code.

Put yourself in the others' shoes: This is not the be-all and end-all of journalistic principles, but it does sometimes enable reporters to come to the right conclusions.

Consult: One of the most scary things in journalism is when reporters think that they know it all and that they therefore do not have to consult. Whenever in doubt, talk to your peers and your seniors. Two (or more) heads are always better than one. And read. Google. Whatever. Just make sure. Rather be safe than sorry.

Most common mistakes

What follows, is a list of the most common breaches of the Press Code that I have encountered in my just over three years as Ombudsman (after handling more than 700 complaints). I include this in the hope that this would help journalists take care not to repeat them. I do this roughly in the way that they most commonly occur.

Not asked for comment: I would not have believed it if anybody told me so – but in my experience more that 90% of all complaints lodged with my office include this complaint.

Inaccurate reporting: Mainly because of the above (but not exclusively so), the second most common mistake is inaccurate reporting. Whatever has happened to checking and verifying facts, I simply do not know.

Anonymous sources: Some politicians (and other people) try to take advantage of journalists and discredit their opponents purposefully under the guise of anonymity. Some journalists fall for it.

One source only, lack of verification: Stories that are likely to harm somebody should be based on more than one source – which in too many cases do not happen. Often, journalists do not verify information that is likely to harm somebody; they also frequently neglect to state that they were not able to verify their information. All too often they merely repeat inaccurate statements that were reported earlier.

Stating opinions/allegations as fact: Many times journalists start off well by attributing their information to sources. However, they often stop doing that the longer the story gets. Eventually readers cannot be blamed for interpreting these texts as statements of fact rather than somebody's opinion. Other times, sub-editors need to shorten the story and think that it is in order to delete the attributions.

Omitted, to suit (bias): Sometimes journalists only use information from press releases, documents or written responses to questions that suits their agendas; they then simply leave out material information that is not to their liking.

Out of context: Some journalists do not understand the importance of context and do not realise that it is as important as text.

Assumptions: Often, journalists make assumptions that are not always necessarily correct and accurate.

007: I call this the 007 syndrome, after James Bond – who infamously has a "license to kill". Unfortunately, there are some journalists and publications who believe that certain people and organisations are evil and that they therefore have this "license to kill". These journalists then lose perspective, believing that they have *carte blanche* to write anything they like (these pet enemies are bad, so whatever we write about them must be right…).

Tick-boxes

Here are some tick-boxes that may help journalists to ensure that their work is ethical. Not every issue would be applicable in every instance – so you decide.

For story-writing journalists	Yes	No	N/A
Have I striven for truth ?			
Is my story likely to unnecessarily cause harm ?			
Has any outside influence tinted my reporting ?			
Did I obtain my information legally, honestly and fairly?			
Have I identified myself as a journalist ?			
Did I report my news truthfully, accurately and fairly ?			
Does my story reflect the proper context ?			
Did I attribute information where necessary ?			
Have I verified my information ?			
Have I plagiarized ?			
Dignity, reputation, privacy: Have I taken care ?			
Rape victims, HIV: Have I taken care ?			
Did I discriminate or commit hate speech ?			
Children: Did I take exceptional care ?			
Violence: Did I take care ?			

Did I protect anonymous sources ?			
Have I tried to avoid the use of anonymous sources ?			
Have I unnecessarily paid for information ?			

For sub-editing journalists	Yes	No	N/A
Is it possible that the writer did not strive for truth ?			
Is the story likely to unnecessarily cause harm ?			
May outside influences have tinted the reporting ?			
Was the information obtained legally, honestly, fairly ?			
Is the story truthful, accurate and fair ?			
Does the story reflect the proper context ?			
Is the information attributed ?			
Are you satisfied that the information was verified ?			
Dignity, reputation, privacy: Has care ben taken ?			
Rape victims, HIV: Has care been taken ?			
Does the story discriminate or commit hate speech ?			
Children: Did the writer take exceptional care ?			
Violence: Did the writer take care ?			
Does my headline, caption reasonably reflect the story ?			
Does the picture misrepresent the story ?			

Was the picture manipulated ?			
Does the poster reasonably reflect the story ?			

For column-writing journalists	Yes	No	N/A
Was my comment honestly and fairly made ?			
Is it clear that my comment is comment ?			
Is my comment made on facts truly stated ?			
Is there any malice in my comment ?			
Did I take fair account of all available, material facts ?			
Have I distorted any facts ?			

Conclusion

Here are some thoughts. It may be helpful if, after reading this book, you draw your own conclusions.

- The press has enormous influence;

- This power can either be constructive or destructive – which means that the press can do immeasurable good, or immeasurable harm;

- It the press acts destructively and does harm it must be in the public interest to do so;

- The only responsibility that the press has towards society is to do its job properly;

- Truth is the be-all and end-all of journalism;

- If the press does not stay independent it loses everything that it has – its credibility;

- The need for proper media ethics education and the practical implementation thereof is not negotiable;

- The same goes for self-regulation, to ensure that the reports responsibly and stays accountable to the public;

- In turn, this makes a Press Code indispensable; and

- Journalists should serve society and not themselves.

Éthique et Déontologie

Bruno Albin

Les lecteurs, auditeurs, téléspectateurs, les internautes, font de moins en moins confiance à la presse. Le phénomène est observé, très largement. La méfiance s'installe.

Cela se produit au moment où, bien au contraire, le flux toujours grandissant de l'information, conséquence de la mondialisation des événements, rend chaque jour plus nécessaire la présence, le travail du journaliste pour aider à la présentation, à l'explication, au décryptage des nouvelles.

Crise de confiance, donc.

Les journalistes, sont pourtant, le plus souvent, portés par le désir de témoigner pour le public de la presse. Et pour ce faire, ils se réfèrent à des principes professionnels.

Pour remplir leur mission d'information, pour exercer le pouvoir (et le devoir) de dire, de chercher puis de rapporter ce dont ils ont été les témoins, ils empruntent un chemin bien étroit : ce chemin serpente entre leurs propres faiblesses, professionnelles ou humaines d'une part, et d'autre part, les contraintes que l'on tente de leur imposer ou qui se dressent devant eux, plus simplement.

Ils essaient donc de ne pas trébucher, de ne pas buter sur leurs propres erreurs. Ils essaient aussi de contourner les obstacles que l'on dresse, ici ou là, autour d'eux, pour limiter leur accès à l'information.

Pour atteindre leur but, les journalistes se sont dotés d'un système de références : la déontologie. Ils l'utilisent pour ne pas sortir de l'itinéraire professionnel qu'ils suivent jour après jour. Et ils en ont grand besoin.

Le cadre légal en France

En France, les lois définissent le cadre dans lequel les journalistes exercent leur profession. Par exemple, certains textes disent *« qui »* peut se prévaloir de la qualité de journaliste.

Depuis 1935, selon le Code du Travail,

« est journaliste professionnel toute personne qui a pour activité principale, régulière et rétribuée, l'exercice de sa profession (…) et qui en tire le principal de ses ressources ».

Ce professionnel-là exerce sa profession. Mais la définition de la profession manque.

Pour la Liberté de la Presse, les textes sont plus clairs. Le jeudi 1er octobre 1789, la Déclaration des Droits de l'Homme et du Citoyen affirme en son article 11 que

« la libre communication des pensées et des opinions est un des droits les plus précieux de l'Homme. Tout citoyen peut donc parler, écrire, imprimer librement, sauf à répondre de l'abus de cette liberté dans les cas déterminés par la Loi ».

L'Histoire de la Révolution va montrer que les choses ne sont pas si simples…

Presque cent ans et quelques révolutions plus tard, la grande Loi du 29 juillet 1881[1] sur la liberté de la presse dispose d'abord, en son article 5, que *« tout journal ou écrit périodique peut être publié, sans autorisation préalable et sans dépôt de cautionnement ».*

Mais cette loi, historique, plusieurs fois révisée et qui demeure le texte fondamental de la République française en matière de presse, a une forte connotation pénale.

---

1   *http://www.legifrance.gouv.fr/affichTexte.do?cidTexte=LEGITEXT000006070722&dateTexte=20080312*

Et après avoir affirmé la Liberté, elle l'encadre. Elle précise ainsi, au fil des ans, les grands principes que le journaliste ne peut enfreindre parmi lesquels, l'impératif d'exactitude de l'information, le droit de réponse, la diffamation des personnes, l'injure, la protection des mineurs.

Pourtant, pas plus que la loi de 1935 ne définit la profession, la loi de 1881 de dit véritablement les droits et les devoirs des journalistes. Les journalistes eux-mêmes se sont mis au travail pour tenter de définir l'essentiel.

En juillet 1918 le tout jeune Syndicat national des journalistes, fondé en pleine Guerre Mondiale publie un premier texte, une vraie référence pour la déontologie professionnelle.

Ce premier texte qui s'adresse aux journalistes français touche à l'essentiel en matière de journalisme. C'est une *« charte »* des *« devoirs professionnels »* qui s'imposent à *« un journaliste digne de ce nom »*.

La charte sera révisée en 1938, puis en 2011. C'est la référence la plus largement considérée aujourd'hui en France.

Charte d'éthique professionnelle des journalistes

Syndicat national des journalistes, 1918 - 38 - 2011

Le droit du public à une information de qualité, complète, libre, indépendante et pluraliste, rappelé dans la Déclaration des droits de l'homme et la Constitution française, guide le journaliste dans l'exercice de sa mission. Cette responsabilité vis-à-vis du citoyen prime sur toute autre.

Ces principes et les règles éthiques ci-après engagent chaque journaliste, quelles que soient sa fonction, sa responsabilité au sein de la chaîne éditoriale et la forme de presse dans laquelle il exerce.
Cependant, la responsabilité du journaliste ne peut être confondue avec celle de l'éditeur, ni dispenser ce dernier de ses propres obligations.
Le journalisme consiste à rechercher, vérifier, situer dans son contexte, hiérarchiser, mettre en forme, commenter et publier une information de qualité ; il ne peut se confondre avec la communication. Son exercice demande du temps et des moyens, quel que soit le support. Il ne peut y avoir de respect des règles déontologiques sans mise en œuvre des conditions d'exercice qu'elles nécessitent.
La notion d'urgence dans la diffusion d'une information ou d'exclusivité ne doit pas l'emporter sur le sérieux de l'enquête et la vérification des sources.

La sécurité matérielle et morale est la base de l'indépendance du journaliste. Elle doit être assurée, quel que soit le contrat de travail qui le lie à l'entreprise.
L'exercice du métier à la pige bénéficie des mêmes garanties que celles dont disposent les journalistes mensualisés.

Le journaliste ne peut être contraint à accomplir un acte ou exprimer une opinion contraire à sa conviction ou sa conscience professionnelle, ni aux principes et règles de cette charte.
Le journaliste accomplit tous les actes de sa profession (enquête, investigations, prise d'images et de sons, etc.) librement, a accès à toutes les sources d'information concernant les faits qui conditionnent la vie publique et voit la protection du secret de ses sources garantie.

C'est dans ces conditions qu'un journaliste digne de ce nom :
– Prend la responsabilité de toutes ses productions professionnelles, mêmes anonymes ;
– Respecte la dignité des personnes et la présomption d'innocence ;
– Tient l'esprit critique, la véracité, l'exactitude, l'intégrité, l'équité, l'impartialité, pour les piliers de l'action journalistique ; tient l'accusation sans preuve, l'intention de nuire, l'altération des documents, la déformation des faits, le détournement d'images, le mensonge, la manipulation, la censure et l'autocensure, la non vérification des faits, pour les plus graves dérives professionnelles ;
– Exerce la plus grande vigilance avant de diffuser des informations d'où qu'elles viennent ;
– Dispose d'un droit de suite, qui est aussi un devoir, sur les informations qu'il diffuse et fait en sorte de rectifier rapidement toute information diffusée qui se révèlerait inexacte ;
– N'accepte en matière de déontologie et d'honneur professionnel que la juridiction de ses pairs ; répond devant la justice des délits prévus par la loi ;
– Défend la liberté d'expression, d'opinion, de l'information, du commentaire et de la critique ;
– Proscrit tout moyen déloyal et vénal pour obtenir une information. Dans le cas où sa sécurité, celle de ses sources ou la gravité des faits l'obligent à taire sa qualité de journaliste, il prévient sa hiérarchie et en donne dès que possible explication au public ;
– Ne touche pas d'argent dans un service public, une institution ou une entreprise privée où sa qualité de journaliste, ses influences, ses relations seraient susceptibles d'être exploitées ;
– N'use pas de la liberté de la presse dans une intention intéressée ;
– Refuse et combat, comme contraire à son éthique professionnelle, toute confusion entre journalisme et communication ;
– Cite les confrères dont il utilise le travail, ne commet aucun plagiat ;
– Ne sollicite pas la place d'un confrère en offrant de travailler à des conditions inférieures ;
– Garde le secret professionnel et protège les sources de ses informations ;
– Ne confond pas son rôle avec celui du policier ou du juge.

Déclaration des droits de l'homme et du citoyen (article XI) : « *Le libre communication des pensées et des opinions est un des droits les plus précieux de l'Homme : tout Citoyen peut donc parler, écrire, imprimer librement, sauf à répondre de l'abus de cette liberté, dans les cas déterminés par la Loi.* »

Constitution de la France (article 34) : « *La loi fixe les règles concernant les droits civiques et les garanties fondamentales accordées aux citoyens pour l'exercice des libertés publiques ; la liberté, le pluralisme et l'indépendance des médias.* » Déclaration des devoirs et des droits des journalistes (Munich, 1971) : le SNJ, qui fut à l'initiative de la création de la Fédération Internationale des Journalistes, en 1926 à Paris, est également l'un des inspirateurs de cette Déclaration qui réunit l'ensemble des syndicats de journalistes au niveau européen.

Syndicat National des Journalistes – 33, rue du Louvre 75002, – www.snj.fr, email : snj@snj.fr, – tél : 01 42 36 84 23, fax : 01 45 08 80 33

La charte de Munich 1971

La nécessité de disposer d'un véritable cadre de référence se manifeste à travers toute l'Europe. C'est une initiative de l'Union des journalistes allemands qui va conduire, en 1971, à l'adoption de la Charte de Munich par la Fédération européenne des journalistes. En tête, elle affirme dix devoirs suivis de cinq droits.

Préambule

Le droit à l'information, à la libre expression et à la critique est une des libertés fondamentales de tout être humain. De ce droit du public à connaître les faits et les opinions procède l'ensemble des devoirs et des droits des journalistes.

La responsabilité des journalistes vis-à-vis du public prime toute autre responsabilité, en particulier à l'égard de leurs employeurs et des pouvoirs publics.

La mission d'information comporte nécessairement des limites que les journalistes eux-mêmes s'imposent spontanément. Tel est l'objet de la déclaration des devoirs formulée ici. Mais ces devoirs ne peuvent être effectivement respectés dans l'exercice de la profession de journaliste que si les conditions concrètes de l'indépendance et de la dignité professionnelle sont réalisées. Tel est l'objet de la déclaration des droits qui suit.

Déclaration des devoirs

1. Respecter la vérité, quelles qu'en puissent être les conséquences pour lui-même, et ce, en raison du droit que le public a de connaître la vérité.

2. Défendre la liberté de l'information, du commentaire et de la critique.

3. Publier seulement les informations dont l'origine est connue ou dans le cas contraire les accompagner des réserves nécessaires; ne pas supprimer les informations essentielles et ne pas altérer les textes et documents.

4. Ne pas user de méthodes déloyales pour obtenir des informations, des photographies et des documents.

125

5. S'obliger à respecter la vie privée des personnes.

6. Rectifier toute information publiée qui se révèle inexacte.

7. Garder le secret professionnel et ne pas divulguer la source des informations obtenues confidentiellement.

8. S'interdire le plagiat, la calomnie, la diffamation et les accusations sans fondement, ainsi que de recevoir un quelconque avantage en raison de la publication ou de la suppression d'une information.

9. Ne jamais confondre le métier de journaliste avec celui du publicitaire ou du propagandiste; n'accepter aucune consigne, directe ou indirecte, des annonceurs.

10. Refuser toute pression et n'accepter de directive rédactionnelle que des responsables de la rédaction.

Tout journaliste digne de ce nom se fait un devoir d'observer strictement les principes énoncés ci-dessus. Reconnaissant le droit en vigueur dans chaque pays, le journaliste n'accepte en matière d'honneur professionnel que la juridiction de ses pairs, à l'exclusion de toute ingérence gouvernementale ou autre.

Déclaration des droits

1. Les journalistes revendiquent le libre accès à toutes les sources d'information et le droit d'enquêter librement sur tous les faits qui conditionnent la vie publique. Le secret des affaires publiques ou privées ne peut en ce cas être opposé au journaliste que par exception et en vertu de motifs clairement exprimés.

2. Le journaliste a le droit de refuser toute subordination qui serait contraire à la ligne générale de l'organe d'information auquel il collabore, telle qu'elle est déterminée par écrit dans son contrat d'engagement, de même que toute subordination qui ne serait pas clairement impliquée par cette ligne générale.

3. Le journaliste ne peut être contraint à accomplir un acte professionnel ou à exprimer une opinion qui serait contraire à sa conviction ou à sa conscience.

4. L'équipe rédactionnelle doit être obligatoirement informée de toute décision importante de nature à affecter la vie de l'entreprise. Elle doit être au moins consultée, avant toute décision définitive, sur toute mesure intéressant la composition de la rédaction : embauche, licenciement, mutation et promotion des journalistes.

5. En considération de sa fonction et de ses responsabilités, le journaliste a droit non seulement au bénéfice des conventions collectives, mais aussi à un contrat personnel assurant la sécurité matérielle et morale de son travail ainsi qu'à une rémunération correspondant au rôle social qui est le sien, et suffisante pour garantir son indépendance économique.

On le voit, les journalistes situent leurs devoirs avant les droits qu'ils revendiquent.

Mais ces chartes, telles que l'envisagent les journalistes, ne s'imposent pas à tous. Elles sont d'abord considérées comme une déclaration assez solennelle de principes professionnels qui devraient s'imposer à l'ensemble de la profession. Leur raison d'être, c'est l'affirmation de valeurs. Mais dans les faits, ces valeurs, ces principes, dont certains touchent aux pouvoirs des éditeurs de journaux, ont tardé à être pris formellement en considération.

Il n'y a pas de charte déontologique commune en France. Il n'y a pas non plus de Conseil de la Presse, organe qui existe pourtant dans de nombreux pays européens : l'Allemagne, la Suisse, le Royaume-Uni, le Luxembourg, et aussi le Canada, le Bénin, le Burkina Faso, etc. Pas de Médiateur National de la Presse en France, comme c'est le cas en Afrique du Sud par exemple.

On pourrait presque dire comme on le disait au moment du débat parlementaire sur le texte qui allait donner naissance à la loi de 1881, qu'en France, « désormais, le déontologue, c'est le juge ».

Vers la création d'une instance déontologique

Et pourtant, les journalistes français ressentent l'obligation de progresser dans cette direction. En 2009, une négociation entre les journalistes et les éditeurs a échoué. Chacun a rejeté la responsabilité de cet échec sur l'autre.

Peut-être y a-t-il, de façon sous-jacente, une raison qui tient à l'histoire. En France, mais aussi ailleurs, le droit de la presse a été sérieusement restreint par des textes de loi extrêmement contraignants. Au dix-neuvième siècle, il y a l'autorisation préalable de la publication d'un journal et la censure. Cela laisse des traces. Et chez certains patrons de presse, comme un atavisme professionnel, l'idée bien ancrée que les principes professionnels sont le pain quotidien des « déontologues ». L'expression est passablement méprisante.

Malgré l'échec de 2009, les organisations professionnelles ne désarment pas : le Syndicat National des Journalistes (SNJ) a annoncé, le 5 octobre dernier, lors de son congrès, qu'il souhaite le lancement d'une nouvelle action, en vue de la création d'une instance déontologique de la profession. Et il souligne l' urgence d'y parvenir.

> « Le droit du public à une information de qualité, complète, libre, indépendante et pluraliste guide le journaliste dans l'exercice de sa mission. Cette responsabilité vis-à-vis du citoyen prime sur toute autre », rappelle la Charte d'éthique professionnelle des journalistes (SNJ, 1918/38/2011).

> Alors que la défiance, voire l'indifférence, du public envers les médias ne cesse de croître, c'est dans cet esprit (…) que le SNJ (…) appelle à la création d'une instance déontologique. Seul un geste fort montrant la volonté de l'ensemble de la profession de se prendre en mains est à même d'inverser cette tendance et de contribuer à regagner la confiance des lecteurs de la presse papier ou numérique, des auditeurs et des

téléspectateurs. Structure composée essentiellement de professionnels, elle devra cependant associer des représentants de la société civile à cette réflexion. »

Cette initiative qui vise à « regagner la confiance » du public est saluée par les professionnels réunis dans l'APCP, l'Association de Préfiguration d'un Conseil de Presse et au-delà.

Mais l'horizon de la déontologie des journalistes a ceci de commun avec celui de la démocratie : quelle que soit la distance parcourue dans la bonne direction, l'horizon recule toujours.

Les codes de déontologie

Les codes de déontologie font néanmoins partie du quotidien des journalistes. De nombreux journaux ont adopté leur propre code, le plus souvent inspiré des textes et des Chatres déjà existants.

L'audiovisuel

Les médias audiovisuels français, sont placés sous l'autorité d'une instance de régulation, le Conseil Supérieur de l'Audiovisuel (CSA). Cette instance est l'héritière en quelque sorte de deux autres organismes : la Haute Autorité de la Communication Audiovisuelle (1982-1986) et à la Commission nationale de la communication et des libertés (1986-1989). Antérieurement, la gestion de l'Audiovisuel en France était organisée sous l'autorité d'un ministre et donc, du pouvoir exécutif.

L'interventionnisme décrié du pouvoir politique auprès des médias publics a conduit en 1982 à la création de ces instances «indépendantes».

Le CSA s'assure du respect des règles déontologiques de l'information et des programmes. Il s'appuie notamment sur les textes légaux en vigueur, et singulièrement sur la Loi du 29 juillet 1881:

- Respect de la dignité de la personne humaine
- Sauvegarde de l'ordre public
- Santé publique
- Lutte contre les discriminations
- Honnêteté et indépendance de l'Information
- Traitement des affaires judiciaires
- Respect du droit à la vie privée

Journalistes, audiovisuel et déontologie : Les engagements de la télévision publique en France

France Télévisions, la télévision publique française s'est dotée d'une Charte des Antennes. Les journalistes de différentes chaînes et le public y trouvent les principes fondamentaux que le Groupe France Télévisions s'impose, notamment dans le traitement de l'actualité. Les sujets abordés sont ceux, communs à la plupart des chartes ou Codes de déontologie. Mais le document va très loin dans le détail des écueils à éviter et des réflexes professionnels à acquérir en vue l'exercice quotidien de la profession.

Plutôt que de se référer à la notion d'objectivité de l'information que personne n'est jamais réellement parvenu à définir, la Charte de France Télévisions lui préfère celle d'honnêteté de l'information.

L'honnêteté de l'information

L'honnêteté est l'exigence fondamentale de la télévision publique en matière d'information.

Elle requiert une information :

- *exacte, conforme à la réalité, qui proscrit toute présentation partiale des faits ;*

- *qui implique la vérification et le sérieux des sources d'information;*

- *qui traite avec la plus grande prudence les informations incertaines, refuse de tenir pour avérées des affirmations personnelles ou fondées sur la rumeur publique, non confirmées par des sources vérifiées et concordantes ;*

- *qui exige rigueur et précision de la langue, du traitement de l'information et de sa présentation, qui bannit l'approximation.*

C'est après ce rappel indispensable des principes fondateurs de la déontologie professionnelle que la Charte de l'Antenne de France Télévisions entre dans le vif du sujet.

Elle répond dans le détail au questionnement récurrent des journalistes face à la complexité de leur outil et à la rapidité de la transmission des nouvelles : il est donc intéressant de noter le souci apporté à la description des risques encourus dans le traitement de l'information sous le double effet de l'abondance des éléments d'information et des contraintes liées à ce traitement dans l'urgence.

Avec l'émergence des nouvelles techniques de traitement et de transmission de l'image, la multiplication des sources d'informations et d'images, ainsi que le développement d'images de vidéastes amateurs, l'émergence des réseaux sociaux et des «lanceurs d'alerte», une vigilance particulière s'impose.

Le besoin constant d'images et les conditions d'urgence dans lesquelles les rédactions sont souvent amenées à opérer, créent un environnement propice à la survenance de manquements préjudiciables à la crédibilité de l'information.

Les moyens techniques permettent de rendre compte des événements en temps réel, mais « en aucun cas la notion d'urgence ne doit l'emporter sur le sérieux de l'enquête et sur la vérification des sources».

4.2. Les sources d'information et leur qualité

Toute information doit être vérifiée avant d'être présentée à l'antenne. France Télévisions ne diffusera pas de nouvelle non vérifiée sous la seule pression de l'événement.

Il importe, avant la diffusion, de connaître :

- *la crédibilité et l'autorité de la source ;*
- *son intérêt dans la publication de l'information ;*
- *l'implication de la source, directe ou indirecte, et ses motivations;*
- *les sources réelles des informations recueillies sur les réseaux de l'internet qui subissent des reprises multiples, et de les recouper;*
- *les informations doivent être recoupées dans la mesure du possible avec d'autres sources indépendantes ;*
- *si les recoupements ne sont pas immédiatement possibles ou satisfaisants et si les rédactions jugent que l'information doit être malgré tout portée à la connaissance du public, elle sera présentée sous forme dubitative ou/ et en précisant la source.*

Les moteurs de recherche sur l'Internet ne doivent pas être considérés comme des fournisseurs de sources fiables. Ils ne donnent que des pistes de recherche.

4.3. Les images

Toute image doit être vérifiée avant d'être présentée à l'antenne.

France Télévisions diffuse essentiellement des images dont la source est connue, vérifiée et crédible – chaînes de télévision, agences d'images avec lesquelles elle a passé des accords.

Toute image disponible sur l'Internet, y compris sur les réseaux sociaux, ne peut être considérée a priori comme libre de droits. Il est indispensable d'identifier le titulaire qui peut être :

- *un producteur ;*
- *une agence ;*
- *un particulier.*
- *Certaines images ou documents peuvent être disponibles sous réserve de licences type « creative commons ». Si nécessaire, les droits doivent être acquis pour les exploitations envisagées par France Télévisions. Les images sont visionnées au préalable et présentées dans un souci de mise en contexte et d'explication.*

- *L'abondance des sources impose toutes les formes de clarification : identification, par des mentions incrustées, du statut de la séquence, de la nature des éléments présentés, etc. Toute utilisation d'images d'archives est précisée par une incrustation à l'écran (lieu et date, heure si nécessaire, mention d'archives avec leur date de réalisation).*

- *Les images issues de l'internet doivent porter la mention de leur source.*

- *Les images fournies par des sociétés extérieures [par exemple, les images de produits fournies par des entreprises qui n'ont pas autorisé de tournage indépendant] doivent être clairement identifiées.*

- *Si une image est douteuse, présente un risque de manipulation ou a pour but de diffuser une propagande, mais est jugée d'intérêt public, il sera fait mention de sa source et des motifs de sa diffusion.*

- *Les reconstitutions de faits réels sont mentionnées comme telles.*

- *Les journalistes veillent à l'adéquation entre les images diffusées et les sujets qu'elles sont censées illustrer, et à ne pas les détourner de leur finalité.*

- *France Télévisions veille au respect du droit à l'image des personnes (cf. chapitre 2, p. 23).*

- *Les journalistes sont tenus de respecter toute clause particulière, contrat ou décision de justice, attachée à ces images.*

Le téléspectateur doit toujours être en mesure de connaître la nature et l'origine des images qui lui sont présentées. Il est donc important de faire à l'antenne une distinction claire entre les genres, par exemple entre information et divertissement. Il faut annoncer clairement au téléspectateur ce qu'il va regarder : un reportage, une reconstitution, une fiction, etc.

La Charte des Antennes de France Télévisions dresse ainsi une liste extrêmement détaillée des questions déontologiques auxquelles les journalistes doivent savoir trouver des réponses.

- La maîtrise du montage

- L'anonymat des sources et sa protection

- Le recours aux enregistrements caméra cachée : « uniquement pour les nécessités de l'information du public (…) dans les limites imposées par la loi : les équipes doivent respecter la dignité de la personne, le droit à la vie privée et à l'image »

- La hiérarchie, l'approfondissement et le suivi de l'information

- Le traitement des questions judiciaires. (Cette question est essentielle dans une société où l'instrumentalisation des média se banalise, où le secret de l'instruction est bafoué par les avocats et les magistrats eux-mêmes.)

- Le droit des victimes

- La protection des mineurs délinquants

- Les comptes-rendus judiciaires

France Télévisions a également créé la fonction de médiateur, dont le rôle est d'être l'intermédiaire entre le public et les chaînes. Les médiateurs sont nommés pour trois ans, indépendants de toute hiérarchie, ils ont accès à l'antenne et peuvent être responsables, et même seuls responsables d'une émission régulière dont ils composent eux-mêmes le contenu et à laquelle ils invitent quiconque leur paraît susceptible d'éclairer le point de vue du téléspectateur.

L'éthique du journaliste

On le voit, il ne manque pas de textes, de déclarations, de chartes ni de codes en matière de déontologie professionnelle. L'idée qui prévaut souvent chez les journalistes est que le sujet est trop sérieux pour que l'on demande à des « non journalistes » d'intervenir dans la rédaction d'une charte unique, ou d'un code de déontologie pouvant s'appliquer à minima, de façon uniforme, à l'ensemble de la profession.

Mais il faut opposer aux dérapages malheureusement spectaculaires de la profession une volonté d'analyser et de sanctionner les fautes professionnelles caractérisées. Ce n'est pas toujours le cas.

Les journalistes français ont en mémoire deux affaires qui ont défrayé la chronique, créé le scandale et n'ont été suivies d'aucune mesure, d'aucune sanction véritable.

La première remonte à une vingtaine d'années. Un journaliste, présentateur vedette de l'une des chaînes de télévision privées, a diffusé, dans son journal, le 16 décembre 1991, une interview de Fidel Castro prétendument réalisée à Cuba. Il est simple de comprendre ce scandale : l'interview en question n'a jamais été réalisée par le « journaliste » en question. Il s'agit d'un montage : les questions étaient posées, pendant une conférence de presse, par une journaliste argentine, et les « questions » filmées, après la conférence de presse reprenaient plus ou moins celles de la journaliste en question. Cette vraie « fausse interview » a fait scandale. Mais le présentateur a continué à présenter ses journaux.

La seconde affaire est celle d'Outreau, une commune du Nord de la France où l'annonce de l'ouverture d'une instruction judiciaire dans une affaire d'abus sexuels sur mineurs aboutit à l'une des erreurs judiciaires les plus spectaculaires de l'histoire judiciaire récente. Les accusés presque tous condamnés au terme d'un premier procès sont tous acquittés en appel. La Justice sort salie de cette affaire. Le ministre présentera des excuses publiques. Une commission d'enquête parlementaire tentera de démonter le mécanisme de cette tragédie. Le rôle de la presse, qui, d'une façon générale, a tout relayé, est largement commenté, critiqué. Sans que cela débouche vraiment sur une remise en cause profonde.

On est bien loin des principes énoncés par les Chartes professionnelles que nous venons d'évoquer. Et à l'heure où nous nous penchons sur la pratique déontologique du journalisme et sur l'éthique de cette profession, c'est à la BBC, à Londres, que le scandale éclate.

L'émission *NewsNight* vient de présenter le témoignage d'un homme accusant un homme politique, identifié comme un ancien trésorier du Parti Conservateur, de l'avoir sexuellement abusé à plusieurs reprises lorsqu'il était pensionnaire d'une institution pour mineurs. L'accusateur s'est depuis rétracté. Mais l'affaire a conduit le directeur général de la BBC à démissionner.

Il n'en faut pas plus pour faire ressurgir en Grande Bretagne l'exigence de la création d'une instance de régulation «indépendante». La demande vient de la numéro deux du Parti travailliste Harriet Harman. En gros dit-elle, les politiciens doivent s'occuper de ce que les journalistes n'ont pas su faire seuls. Et un sondage du « Guardian » prend tout son sens : 83% des personnes ayant répondu à un questionnaire du journal se prononcent en faveur d'une « *régulation organisée légalement* ». Seule une petite minorité de lecteurs souhaitent qu'on laisse aux journalistes le soin de pratiquer la « *self-regulation* » ayant cours aujourd'hui.

Les journalistes habitués à se pencher sur ces questions comprennent bien l'agacement parfois, la colère souvent, de l'opinion publique.

On sait bien, dans toutes les rédactions, pour avoir étudié, ou réfléchi à ces questions où se trouve la ligne de partage entre ce qui est admissible dans la pratique professionnelle et ce qui ne l'est pas.

On l'a vu, il ne manque pas de références, de chartes et de codes. Principes clairement rassemblés. Certains vont à l'essentiel. D'autres détaillent les textes avec le souci de baliser en quelque sorte le chemin à suivre pour ne pas tomber dans l'erreur.

Personne évidemment n'emporte avec lui en reportage le Code de déontologie de son journal. Très rares sont ceux qui peuvent, de mémoire, dire les 15 articles de la Charte de Munich. Mais il y en a sans doute.

Pourtant, tous doivent avoir pour bagage le désir individuel, personnel, de se comporter d'une façon juste, raisonnée, d'une façon éthique.

La matière première du journalisme, c'est la vie.

Aucun code de déontologie ne peut véritablement couvrir toutes les situations de la vie dans la perspective de la pratique professionnelle. D'abord, parce qu'un Code, c'est un texte, dont tous les mots comptent, certes, mais un texte imprimé auquel on ne peut pas retrancher la moindre virgule. C'est une somme faite de bon sens et d'expérience. Mais c'est une somme qui doit tomber juste.

Le Code n'intègre pas ce qui surgit, inopinément, comme par surprise. Une situation totalement nouvelle, pour moi, en tout cas. Un univers culturel que je découvre et auquel ma propre culture ne m'a pas préparé. Une rencontre que je ne pouvais imaginer. Une idée qui me révolte autant qu'elle me semble devoir être présentée au public. Le Code n'intègre pas ma sensibilité. Mais c'est ma sensibilité qui donnera, peut-être, du prix à mon reportage.

Tout ce qui est dans le Code, que je ne peux emporter avec moi pour le consulter, tout cela qui nourrit ma conscience de journaliste, et toute ma culture, tout cela forme un système de référence personnel, l'éthique, le sens éthique qui m'accompagne dans toute la vie professionnelle. L'éthique, vivante, et qui sait m'aider à choisir un comportement professionnel juste et humain au moment où les Chartes et les Codes semblent ne plus pouvoir répondre à mes interrogations, à mes doutes.

La qualité, la formation

La meilleure façon de se prémunir contre la volonté de certains de définir la déontologie du journalisme à la place des journalistes eux-mêmes, c'est d'offrir au public une information de qualité.

Le public ne se trompe pas : il faut lui présenter des informations exactes, précises, savoir lui montrer l'importance d'une nouvelle, pouvoir décrypter un événement apparemment le concernant peu et le placer au bon endroit, pour que le lecteur finisse par le faire figurer en bonne place parmi les sujets dignes d'intérêt qui l'aident à mieux comprendre, si cela est possible, la marche du temps et du monde. Tout cela conduit au rapprochement, à une relation de confiance retrouvée entre les journalistes et leur public.

Les Codes de déontologie, les Chartes professionnelles ne sont rien sans la formation, sans le désir d' accomplir au mieux une mission essentielle. L'éthique ne se décrète pas non plus. Elle naît de la rencontre en un savoir et une conscience.

Joseph Pulitzer

Joseph Pulitzer , créateur des Prix qui portent son nom, et qui récompensent chaque année les meilleures productions de l'esprit aux Etats-Unis, et celles du Journalisme en particulier a été un immense Journaliste.

Il paraît qu'il faisait graver un slogan sur les tables de travail de sa rédaction :

> *« Ecrivez court et vous serez lu. Ecrivez clairement et vous serez compris. Ecrivez imagé et vous resterez en mémoire. »*

A la fin de sa vie, il décida d'offrir 2 millions de dollars à l'Université Columbia de New York pour la création d'une école, la Columbia School of Journalism . Un rêve pour apprenti journaliste.

Lors du premier conseil d'administration, il a bien sûr prononcé un discours. Écoutons-le :

> *« Notre République et sa presse graviront ensemble les sommets ou bien elles iront ensemble à leur perte. Une presse compétente, désintéressée… peut protéger cette morale collective de la vertu, sans laquelle un gouvernement populaire n'est qu'une escroquerie et une mascarade. »*

Bibliographie et Références

- Yves Agnès, Manuel de Journalisme, Collection Grands Repères, La Découverte, 2002-2008

- Yves Agnès, Le Grand Bazar de l'Info - pour en finir avec le maljournalisme, Éditions Michalon, 2005

- Réseau Théophraste, Éthique: Quelques Propositions aux Nouveaux Défis Lancés par l'Évolution de la Société de l' Information, http://www.theophraste.org/Ethique-quelques-propositions-face-aux-nouveaux-defis-lances-par-l-evolution-de-la-societe-de-l-information_a5.html

- UNESCO, Normes Professionnelles et Code de Déontologie du Journalisme, http://www.unesco.org/new/fr/communication-and-information/freedom- of-expression/professional-journalistic--standards-and-code-of-ethics

- Université Panthéon Assas : IFP Droit et Déontologie des Médias, Programme de cours et références bibliographiques, http://ifp.u-paris2.fr/89555084/0/fiche_cours/&RH=IFP-LICENCE

MEDIA EDUCATION FOR GENDER EQUITABLE DEVELOPMENT

Sheila Bunwaree

The Beijing Platform of Action, adopted unanimously by 189 member states of the United Nations at the Fourth World Conference on Women in 1995, had acknowledged the media as one of the twelve critical areas of concern and intervention for women's advancement. Paying attention to media and particularly to gender in the media, was not seen as important in the early years of the International Women's Movement. What were generally seen as priority areas were health, education and poverty, to name but a few. Media was seen as a rather secondary affair, so much so that it was barely given a mention in the strategy documents of the first 3 UN conferences on women. At the time, the inclusion of 'media and communication' in a section of the Beijing document, appeared as a historic moment. In more recent years, there has been increased recognition of the pertinence and role of a gender sensitive media in contributing towards gender equality and more gender inclusive democracies. But despite progress made since 1995, the process remains slow.

As the Beijing Plus 10 process illustrates, media and communication issues continue to exist somewhat on the margins of the International women's agenda. Is it because 'media' remains a highly

141

male dominated arena that breaking through remains very difficult. Callagher notes: *"By 2005, with the World Summit on the Information Society providing a global context for debate on ICTs and development, it might have seemed appropriate to consider media and communications as 'the big thing'- or at least one of the big things - in the official ten year review and appraisal of the Beijing Platform for Action. Yet, astonishingly, media related issues hardly featured in the review proceedings. The whole of media and communications seemed to have fallen off the agenda..."* Needless to say that if media itself fell off the agenda, the debate regarding gender and media would have been further marginalized.

What is interesting and promising however is that some regional groupings across the world continue to see media and ICTs as important areas of intervention for development. The Southern African Development community (SADC) is one such grouping. In August 2008, SADC heads of state and governments signed the groundbreaking SADC protocol on Gender and Development, elevating the SADC declaration to a more binding regional instrument. With its 28 targets, the protocol provides Southern Africa with a road map for the fulfillment of the MDGs...The protocol also has specific targets for media and local government, which includes the equal representation of women in all areas and at all levels of decision making.

The fact that the SADC protocol contains targets for gender and the media seems to indicate that there is a move towards an expanding gender consciousness. But if the latter is about numbers only, the struggle for gender equality would remain a daunting one for a long time to come.

The gender and media baseline study in southern Africa indicate that women are underrepresented in the media. The fact that media houses remain a male dominated space, the chance for gender sensitive materials and reporting to take place remains rather thin. This does not necessarily mean that more women in the media houses would ensure reporting with gender lenses. Improved media training is absolutely vital to remove all the gender biases that prevail and make democracy more equitable. The challenge therefore is to integrate gender awareness training into all types and aspects of media training. This is also part of the mainstreaming exercise.

This paper argues that fighting for an equal representation of women is a necessary but not sufficient condition for gender equitable development and more just democracies. Media content should be revolutionized to make space for gender perspectives. In short media content should be infused with a feminist agenda. For this to happen, every aspect of media training should be genderised.

Mainstreaming gender in the media - from a politics of recognition to a politics of transformation

Mainstreaming gender in the media is not only about increasing the numbers of women in news room, as chief editors, as journalists etc. What is really needed in the media world is a politics of transformation and for this to happen, gender lenses need to be applied in every thing that the media does and/or handles. We need the kind of mainstreaming which ensures that there are more women in particular feminists who write, report, assign, analyse and frame the news. In short gender lenses should be applied to all topics and themes covered in the media. Such gender applications can go a long way in combating gender inequality and assist in attaining MDG goal 3 - that of gender equality - which is reported as the one making the least progress.

Gender in the media in the 2015 post development framework

As we approach 2015 the target year for meeting the MDG goals, there is growing realization that meeting these goals particularly by the developing world would be very difficult if not impossible. The multiplicity of crises - the global financial crisis, the food crisis, the climate change crisis and their interlocking effects have exacerbated many of the problems of the developing world. The resulting feminization of poverty in many places can impact negatively on the attainment of MDG goal 3. But how many journalists, male or female are cognizant of such a situation is a question worth asking.

Leaders across the globe are currently very busy trying to frame the 2015 post development agenda and I wish to suggest that the opportunity of the post 2015 framework be seized to interrogate the role of the media in contributing to make the world a more gender equitable one, a world where human rights are inclusive of women's rights.

The media have become crucial to the workings of the economic, political, social and cultural spheres. The media operates at the local, national and global level as well as in the private sphere, where they are important sources of both information and entertainment.

The media provide spaces in which social, economic, political and cultural issues mentioned above, are presented and discussed but how often are these issues discussed with gender lenses? Gender monitoring of the media undertaken by different civil society groups in diverse spaces show us that this remains rather thin albeit there is some progress. The media plays a significant role in determining which issues will be considered important and legitimate in a society and how they will be defined and discussed. The different forms of media evolving in the world do not simply restrict themselves to the dissemination of messages and nor can one argue that the audience receiving these messages are passive agents. They simply are not. Through the different news and forms of entertainment, the media houses produce and disseminate a wide variety of information, ideas, ways of thinking, assumptions, frameworks, belief systems, values and ethos, narratives. These shape our minds, opinions and world views. The media resources have a huge bearing on us - they shape our understanding and influence our opinion, sometimes they guide our individual actions and activities as well as influence decision making processes and policy formation in the public and political spheres. Thus the media plays an important role in bringing about social change and transformation. But when media is tilted or biased in one direction, it is hard to obtain transformation. Colleen Lowe Morna (2004) aptly notes;

> 'while purporting to reflect society, the media is unrepresentative of society. In southern Africa, women constitute only 20 per cent of all journalists, and less than five per cent of media managers. Within the newsroom, women are glaringly absent from the 'hard' beats such as politics, finance, court and war reporting: the beats most likely to lead to vertical movement, within the media hierarchy.'

The transformative potential of media goes to waste when media remains unrepresentative of society. An 'unrepresentative' media also contributes to the reproduction of inequality and such gender inequality reproduction augurs badly for societies which aspire to become gender inclusive and equitable.

Why is gender and gender inequality important?

The World Development Report 2012 has drawn our attention to the centrality of gender for development and how gender equality matters for development outcomes and policy making. In short gender inequality leads to inefficiency and inequity. Gender inequality arises because of the unequal relations between men and women. Gender inequality means that women are subordinate to men and have less power, fewer resources and fewer opportunities to determine their own lives, as well as the direction of the societies in which they live. Not all women experience gender inequality in the same way because women do not constitute a monolithic, homogenous block. Women vary in terms of age, socioeconomic status, religion, and race. Such diversity also means that gender inequality dynamics play themselves out in different ways.

Whatever be the dynamics, it must be remembered that gender inequality does not simply constitute a 'female' and/or marginal issue but rather represents a crucial problem for society as a whole. Gender inequality has various ramifications and it is bad for any society whatsoever. Gender inequality constitutes a major problem since over 50 per cent of the world's population is not fully contributing to many of the important activities and decision making processes that shape the present and future direction of the planet. The implications of women's low participation (resulting from the pervasive gender inequalities) is that women's lives and the potential for humanity as a whole is being impoverished.

Transformative potential of the media

Despite progress made in various parts of the world, women continue to remain marginalized and vulnerable. This is not to suggest that women do not have 'agency'- women do have agency but they continue to face major stumbling blocks which impact on them negatively. It is therefore important that all institutions including the media play a role to ensure that women who constitute half of humanity be given their rightful place in terms of voice, action and recognition.

Most countries across the world have signed and ratified the convention of all forms of discrimination against women (CEDAW) but when we look at the plight of women especially in the context of the multiplicity of crises, referred to earlier, we find that women's situation is deteriorating in very many parts of the world, In fact, there is concern that gains made so far on gender equality may be eroded. The growing feminization of poverty in an increasingly neo liberal world, whee macro economic policies remain heavily male –biassed, leave little room for transformation. Such a situation calls for a gender sensitive media in all economic matters. What is therefore required is a media which is able to identify and understand the key economic issues and policies affecting women's lives. More on this later but for now, let me turn to some specifics regarding what media should do.

What should the media do?

The media being such an important conveyor of information, communication and entertainment, its transformative potential for a more gender equitable world is enormous. But for that potential to become meaningful, it has to do the following:

1. It has to eliminate gender biases in the media such as subtle and blatant gender stereotypes

2. It has to ensure that it increases women's perspectives - both in terms of sources and content.

3. It has to put an end to gender blind coverage.

4. The use of gender insensitive language has to be stopped.

Issues pertaining to gender equitable development

There are several issues that affect women's lives and that have implications for the making of gender inclusive societies and gender equitable development. Some of these issues include:

- Neoliberalism and macroeconomic policy making

- Fiscal policy and gender blind budgets.

- Climate change and disaster management

- The care economy and the labour market

- The underrepresentation of women in science and technology

- Gender based violence and sexual abuse

The issues mentioned here affect women's lives in myriad ways. It is the male biased policies linked to these very issues that very often contribute to large segments of women becoming assetless, powerless and voiceless. There is no doubt that if media education/ training covers these issues from a gender perspective, the battle for gender equitable development would become easier. Sadly however, the comment made by Lowe Morna some years back is still relevant today. Lowe Morna (2004) wrote:

"The response of media training institutions to glaring gender imbalances has been similar to that of governments that have created a few structures and isolated programmes on gender, or media houses that devote a regular space or time to gender, rather than to grapple with the tougher question of how to make sure a gender perspective runs through all training."

It is important to point out that regular gender monitoring (if done effectively) and if accompanied by proper advocacy and lobby can assist media houses and media training institutions in gearing their work towards greater gender sensitivity as well as transformation.

Conclusion

Gender politics do matter at the simple level of numerical representation, but it is also clear that an uncritical focus on the simple inclusion of women within institutions obscures demands for social justice and political and economic transformation. The mere presence of physical female bodies in institutions will never challenge gender roles and relations if there is no feminist consciousness behind it. What is needed therefore is a multipronged strategy focused on gender balance and gender sensitivity in terms of numbers, content and analysis.

Media training should therefore be revolutionized so that it extends its boundaries from issues of leadership, management, ethics, transparency and accountability to incorporate a whole range of issues such as the ones mentioned above but with a gender perspective so that societies can be truly transformed and human development be enhanced.

GENDER SENSITIVE REPORTING

Christina Chan-Meetoo

"Sex" *refers to the biological and physiological characteristics that define men and women.*

"Gender" *refers to the socially constructed roles, behaviours, activities, and attributes that a given society considers appropriate for men and women.*

World Health Organisation

"Gender" is a word which often raises eyebrows within the journalistic world. It tends to be associated with hysterical feminism; women who come riding high horses to moralise and sanitise news media. However, this is a sad and unproductive belief as gender concepts encompass much more and would clearly be beneficial to all if well understood as tools for contributing to creating a healthier and more equitable society.

But first things first. Let us start by defining the word 'gender'. Gender refers to the characteristics that a society or culture constructs as masculine or feminine. It is deliberately separated from the biological notion of sex which relates to one's physical makeup by referring instead to the social behaviour aspects of human beings. This means that gender is not necessarily fixed, binary or final. Also, although gender has historically been associated with women's movements and still remain largely so, the term now encompasses alternative forms of gender beyond the neat male-female dichotomy to cover LGBT as well (i.e. Lesbians, Gays, Bisexuals and Transsexuals).

According to Judith Butler, gender is performative, that is, it is actively produced within social interactions. Media being an integral part of the process of social construction, it is thus legitimate to explore the gender dimensions of news production and reception. Especially given that the gatekeeping, filtering and agenda-setting aspects of news production set the stage for possible homogenisation of worldviews which are spread within society. The discourses and opinions of some social groups which are amplified by the media have the potential to become tools of power. Voices which seek to challenge the gender status quo often remain unheard or underrepresented. Stereotypes get reinforced and gender representations are reduced to their most simplistic expression. These standardised mental pictures which are conveniently used as shortcuts for simplifying the world unfortunately have far reaching impacts on our worldview and thus need to be debunked.

The workshop on gender-sensitive reporting, which was also held in October 2012, aimed to address such gender-based stereotypes in the media. It provided guidelines on how to become a gender-sensitive reporter. Gender-insensitivity in reporting and language were also highlighted so that participants are aware of this issue.

The production of meaning

According to the media marxists theorists, most media texts contain a 'preferred' or 'dominant' meaning (Hall, 1973). The media serve 'to reinforce a consensual viewpoint by using public idioms and by claiming to voice public opinion' (Woollacott, 1982). The media use their ideological power to reproduce and reinforce the viewpoints of dominant classes as obvious, central and 'natural' (Curran et al, 1982).

Of course, more liberal theorists believe that although there may be intentions inscribed by news producers within their texts, there exist possibilities for the news consumers to create their own alternative or resistant reading (Fiske, 1989 and Hall, 1973) and some even become producers of meaning themselves (notion of 'bricolage' and guerilla tactics by Michel de Certeau, 1980) and activate meanings in texts. For them, the media are potential enablers of ideas and meanings and can thus promote diversity and difference, which may in turn lead to social change.

The question remains though how far the media are using such potential for positive social change.

In this publication, we do not aim to point fingers at news people. Instead, constructive criticism is warranted here as we know full well that individual journalists may not necessarily have a particular gender bias of their own volition. Indeed, we are aware that there are many factors which come into play, to cite a few:

- the individual's upbringing, life experiences and socialisation,

- the policy and editorial line of the media house,

- the economic pressures leading to cost-cutting and thus favouring less expensive forms of reporting with little or no verification,

- the competition for eyeballs leading to sensationalist stories with cheap angles,

- the limited availability of on-the-job training and coaching for young journalists but also for senior journalists to keep abreast of social developments.

Taking all the above in consideration, we thus need to fill the gap in terms of awareness and knowledge about gender issues in general and also understand how to avoid gender biased reporting and ensure there is more attention to gender balance in the news.

"We know that quality journalism is ethical journalism, and that ethical journalism includes full and fair representation of the actions, opinions, concerns and aspirations of women around the world"

(WACC's Deputy General Secretary Lavinia Mohr)

Monitoring of media: some statistics

The most recent source of statistics about gender in the media is the 2010 Southern African Gender and Media Progress Study (GMPS) conducted by Gender Links in several countries of the Southern African region including Mauritius. Although some progress has been noted over the last five years, there is still a long way to go towards achieving balance both in the composition of the newsroom and in the representation of women and their views in the Mauritian media.

Who owns the media and who are top executives?

All of the key owners of leading media houses are men. Although there are more and women in media houses, the number of women in decision-making positions is still very limited (23% women in top management positions) and no big media owner is a woman. To date, all of the four leading daily newspapers (Le Défi Quotidien, L'express, Le Matinal, Le Mauricien) are headed by men and only one woman is editor-in-chief of a weekly out of the four leading weeklies (Week-End, Défi Plus, 5-Plus Dimanche, Le Défi/L'Hebdo). In radio stations, where there used to be one woman editor-in-chief, there is now none.

Neither is there any senior woman journalist in charge of 'serious' talk shows whereas there used to be a few some years ago. Although there are higher numbers of women in the profession, they seem to be generally confined to the lower echelons and be given preference for softer beats and magazine / feature types of programmes focusing on fashion, celebrity and domestic topics.

Who produces the news?

The GMPS notes that there is an increase in the number of women working in media houses, especially in the radio stations. However, the repartition of roles is still largely in favour of the male journalists with 71% of reporters which means that women are given less opportunities to engage in the core journalistic activities (i.e. sourcing, interviewing, writing and editing). This is in contrast to the fact that most TV presenters are women (64%), a position which tends to foreground physical looks over intellect. Women journalists are not in charge of peak hour programmes, especially live news talk shows and phone-in programmes.

Whose voices are heard? How are gender roles represented?

A November 2012 IFJ article states that: *"The 2010 Global Media Monitoring Project revealed a global average of barely one woman in every four people was seen, heard or read about in news stories. This is an improvement from 15 years ago when it was less than one in five. However, the pace is slow."* In Mauritius, the proportion is even lower with a meagre one out of five ratio according to the 2010 Gender and Media Progress Study for Mauritius. Indeed, sources which are used for the production of news stories are overwhelmingly male (81%). The study rightly highlights the fact that many stories use a single source, which in itself is an ethical issue as the practice does not reflect the need for balance in reporting.

The imbalance in terms of the representation of gender roles also remains a live issue as men's voices are most likely to be heard on 'serious' issues such as politics, economics, employment, sustainable development and also sports. Women's voices are most likely to be heard in 'softer' areas and are thus associated to the domestic sphere (about issues linked to the family and the upbringing of children) or specific problematic gender issues (gender violence, sex trade) and beauty-related stories.

Even though there has been an increase in the representation of women as business people, this is often compounded by reference to the subjects as homemakers or to their physical appearance. Not only are women more likely to be used as presenters, they are also more likely to be the subject of graphic depiction as part of the news stories, often with deliberate attempts to choose sexy angles to titillate the news consumer.

According to the 2010 Southern African Gender and Media Progress Study, *"Women are more likely to be identified by a personal tag than men: of the sources identified by a personal tag, women sources make up 20%, such as mother, wife or daughter as compared to 16% of men being identified as father, son or husband."*

Avoiding sexism in language used

As seen above, important issues such as gender are framed by the way language is used by the media. The choice of words and expressions reflects and even reinforces gender power dynamics. Gaye Tuchman denounces the fact that women are typically subjected to symbolic annihilation in the media through under representation (omission) or misrepresentation (trivialisation or condemnation).

Consider the case of the obituary initially published by The New York Times for pioneering rocket scientist Yvonne Brill which started as follows:

> *"She made a mean beef stroganoff, followed her husband from job to job and took eight years off from work to raise three children. "The world's best mom," her son Matthew said. But Yvonne Brill, who died on Wednesday at 88 in Princeton, N.J., was also a brilliant rocket scientist."*

As noted by Jessica Siegel in the Columbia Journalism Review, *"the surprise is the combination of domestic skills with rocket science."* She aptly recalls that the AP Stylebook states: *"Copy should not gratuitously mention family relationships when there is no relevance to the subject. Copy should not express surprise that an attractive woman can be professionally accomplished. Use the same standards for men and women in deciding whether to include specific mention of personal appearance or marital and family situation."*

A careful use of language is necessary in the media. Journalists should strive to use neutral terms as much as possible and avoid assumptions about gender roles. The use of common representations, for example about women being the carers of the family or about the need for them to be beautiful and sexy, only serve to reinforce and legitimate such stereotypes. Also, one can never be too cautious nowadays when making reference to the type of relationships people portrayed in the news are engaged in, for example about marriage or gender of the partner. Assumptions about conventional relationships may misrepresent reality.

> *"[...] language does not merely reflect the way we think: it also shapes our thinking. If words and expressions that imply that women are inferior to men are constantly used, that assumption of inferiority tends to become part of our mindset. Hence the need to adjust our language when our ideas evolve."* (UNESCO Guideline on Gender-Neutral Language, 1999)

A good starting point is the above guide which provides a helpful list of tricks and terms which can be used in order to avoid sexism in language. For example, it advocates the use of neutral or plural forms.

Usual term	May be replaced by
man	person, human being, people, humanity...
businessmen	business people, business executives
chairman	chairperson, president
firemen	firefighters
landlord	owner, proprietor
layman	layperson, novice
salesman	sales representative, shop assistant
spokesman	spokesperson
Mr and Mrs John Smith	Jane and John Smith
Miss and Mrs	Ms

The UNESCO Guideline also recommends the use of punctuation to highlight bias or rewriting as in the following examples:

The husband lets his wife work	The husband 'lets' his wife work
He helps her with the household chores	They share household chores
Dinner will be provided for delegates and their wives	Dinner will be provided for delegates and their spouses/ partners

The French version of the UNESCO Guideline lists the following terms and phrases as being problematic as they carry simplistic assumptions about the gender automatically associated to the functions represented:

- *Les hommes politiques*
- *Les infirmières*

- *La secrétaire*

- *L'homme de loi*

- *Le panier de la ménagère*

- *L'homme de la rue*

- *Les hommes d'affaires*

Women have the right to be treated in the media as individual persons who exist in their own right rather than as someone's other (wife, mother, grandmother, and sister). As such, they should not be depicted as the possessions of husbands or fathers.

Patronising terms such as 'little lady', 'better half' are a total no-no. Similarly, references to little girls as princesses carry the assumption that society expects them to prepare for a lifetime obsession with beauty enhancement tips and cosmetics. As stated by Supreme Court Justice Sonia Sotomayor at a Sesame Street , 'princess' is not a career. Continuous force feeding of stereotypes related to canons of beauty no doubt has a great influence on little girls who are groomed to be avid consumers of cosmetics and beauty enhancement products.

"Every women knows that, regardless of her other achievements, she is a failure if she is not beautiful... The UK beauty industry takes £8.9 billion a year out of women's pockets. Magazines financed by the beauty industry teach little girls that they need make-up and train them to use it, so establishing their lifelong reliance on beauty products."

(Germaine de Greer, 1999)

Covering women in power

The coverage of news related to women who are associated to power circles is unfortunately also quite dichotomous, swinging from one extreme to the other, that is either that of a 'feminine' and caring weaker sex or that of a tough masculinised leader who betrays her feminity.

Partners or spouses of men who are candidates (e.g. Bill Clinton, Nicolas Sarkozy, Barack Obama, Tony Blair) have been regularly subjected to attention of a particular kind which would not necessarily be the case for partners or spouses of women candidates (e.g. Hilary Clinton, Sarah Palin, Ségolène Royal, Angela Merkel). Media coverage has tended to focus on their merit (or lack thereof) as beauty icons, as *"faire-valoir"* during the campaign and even during the mandate in case of success. Women candidates are themselves subjected to extra scrutiny as compared to their male counterparts, often bordering on sexual voyeurism.

Journalists should take care to ensure that their reporting on women candidates, politicians or other public figures does not discriminate on the basis of gender. A good set of questions to be used for testing for discrimination could be:

- Would I report this element if it was a man?

- Would I use the same adjectives and expressions if it was a man?

- Would I present the elements of the news story in the same order if it was a man?

- Would the pictures used be of the same type if it was a man? For instance, am I trying to focus on parts of her body?

On the other hand, women who do succeed are often assumed to be ruthless and to have adopted a male attitude, with the subtext that they are to be viewed with suspicion for having allegedly betrayed their own sex.

As for feminist movements, they tend to be given coverage only for specific occasions flagged as 'women-only' events. The case of the recent movement Femen warrants attention as they are highly sexualised due to their radical use of nudity to promote their views (lately termed 'sextremists') and media people are often too happy to cover the movement's actions without really delving into the ideas related to feminist struggles.

"The permanent reduction of women to their bodies and their sexuality, the negation of their intellectual abilities, the social invisibility of women who cannot please the male gaze: these are keystones of the patriarchal system," writes Mona Chollet in an article entitled 'The fast-food feminism of the topless Femen' in Le Monde Diplomatique.

Eroticisation of news

Such hyper-sexualisation and eroticisation occurs not only for what could be termed women-related stories but also for unrelated news stories such as those focusing on sports, technology and cars for instance. The use of pictures of slim, young, fair-skinned, sexy hostesses presenting latest cars and gadgets is very often gratuitous and destined to 'embellish' the page and titillate the senses of male readers. They also brainwash female readers into believing that they have to strive to resemble these models to be beautiful. The same may be said of celebrity and fashion pages which are loaded with pictures and little text. These pages in newspapers and magazines are an easy pretext for splashing images of semi-nude female bodies in a bid to sell more.

Covering sex-related news stories

As for ordinary people, they are also the victims of discriminatory reporting, especially in cases involving sexual aggression and rape under crime sections (*'faits divers'* in French). There is unfortunately little regard for the protection of the identity of such victims. Even if real names are not cited, often descriptions of place of abode or work, photographies and other clues are carelessly thrown in the report such that identification is made easy. Reporters evoke the fact that the person has given permission to include these in the papers but such victims are often unaware of the possible stigma to which they may further be subjected as a result of media coverage which allows their identification.

Beyond issues of identification, there are also problems of eroticisation and intrusive journalism. The way we speak or write about sexual aggression may affect the perception of the public, blur the line between the victim and the aggressor or encourage voyeurism in the audience. When the victims are inaccessible, reporters may be tempted to rely on third parties (e.g. neighbours, co-workers) to obtain details about the victim and perpetrator, leading to inaccurate reporting with hearsay, rumours and hurtful innuendos. All these result in additional trauma for the victims, especially if coupled with harassment to obtain more information.

> *"[M]edia coverage that is sometimes viewed as insensitive, voyeuristic, and uncaring can compound victims' emotional and psychological suffering. Most crime victims have never before dealt with the news media. They are thrust, often unwillingly, into a limelight they do not seek and do not enjoy solely because of the crimes committed against them. Many victims describe the initial assault from the perpetrator, a secondary assault from the criminal justice system, and a tertiary assault at the hands of the news media. As ABC News and Political Analyst Jeff Greenfield explained in 1986, "What weighs in the scale is not simply the desire of a victim for privacy... but the prospect of further victimization beyond the involuntary thrust into the public arena. And this is something that the journalism community must begin to consider in its daily business.""*
> (Ethics of news media in covering cases of sexual crimes, United States Department of Justice, 2004)

This is not to say that there should not be any coverage of sex-related news stories. Rather than exploit the sensationalist aspects of sex-crime stories, the media can actually play a positive role in society by providing ethical, non-sensationalist coverage. For instance, they can and sometimes do attract the attention of the public to increases in cases of sexual violence, the effectiveness of policies and measures to prevent and reduce such social plagues as well as the network of support which may exist for victims of sexual aggression. In the long run, media coverage can contribute to lifting the veil on hitherto taboo issues and even changes in policy, legislation and law enforcement.

Covering LGBT

As for sexual minorities such as lesbians, gays, bisexuals and transgender, there are no formal statistics about media composition and coverage, possibly due to the persistent taboo around such groups of people in a relatively conservative society. However, a cursory look at coverage shows that they are subjected to the same kind of discrimination as heterosexual women. They are more often than not associated with sexual misbehaviour and sex-crime as victims or perpetrators without necessary caution about identification, right to privacy, eroticisation and voyeurism.

Gender in existing codes of ethics

There is currently only one statutory code of ethics which applies to the broadcasting sector only in Mauritius: the IBA (Independent Broadcasting Authority) Code of Ethics. As for the written press, various associations have proposed codes of conduct without any formal adoption or commitment of the media actors, the latest one being the NEPA (Newspapers Editors and Publishers Association) Code of Conduct. Individual media houses have also adopted their own codes but only La Sentinelle has really publicised its code and set up an internal mechanism for monitoring and mediation for a certain period of time. In Seychelles, there is a national state regulator which has been voted by the National Assembly, the Media Commission, which monitors the media with respect to a code of conduct which was voted in 2010.

The IBA Code of Ethics

There is no specific reference to gender issues in the code apart from the caution to avoid discrimination and offence on the basis of 'race, colour, age, sex, religion, social origin, marital status, physical or mental disability'. It does however state that 'Broadcasters should not add to the distress of people involved in emergencies or personal tragedies' and that portrayal of sexual behaviour and nudity to be contextualised and scheduled appropriately and that there should be no crudity. There is also a specific section for children and the code states that '(...) children under 16 involved in police enquiries or court proceedings relating to sexual offences should not be identified in news or other programmes.' and that 'Due care must be taken over the physical and emotional welfare and the dignity of children who take part or are otherwise involved in programmes.'

The NEPA Code of Conduct

This code also refers to discrimination with respect to ethnic group, caste, colour, creed, sex or sexual orientation and disability. It asks journalists to be careful not to reveal the identity of victims of sexual aggression and prohibits the identification of children aged up to 16 in cases of sexual aggression with special precautions in cases of incests. *"La presse veillera à ne pas révéler l'identité des victimes d'agressions sexuelle et s'abstiendra de publier des informations qui aideraient à leur identification sauf circonstances exceptionnelles."*

Code de Déontologie de la Sentinelle

This internal code has clauses which cover forms of discrimination (race, physical appearance, religion, sex and disability) with a special mention for racist, sexist and homophobic consequences of reporting: *"[Le journaliste] exerce une grande vigilance face à ce qui pourrait provoquer des réactions racistes, sexistes, homophobes, etc."*

It also specifies that identification of victims of sexual aggression should be avoided, especially in the case of minors.

162

The Code of Conduct of the Seychelles Media Commission

The code includes clauses relating to discrimination on the basis of gender and sexual orientation as well as use of offensive language: *'11.1 The Press should avoid prejudicial or pejorative reference to an individual's race, colour, religion, gender, sexual orientation or to any physical or mental illness or disability unless genuinely relevant to the story.'* and *'11.2 The Press should avoid use of offensive language, violence, sex, humiliation and expressions that violate human dignity.'* It advocates the protection of the identity victims of sexual violence: *'12 Victims of sexual assault. The Press should not identify victims of sexual assault or publish material likely to contribute to such identification unless there is adequate justification and they are legally free to do so.'* Further, it has a specific clause labeled Gender Sensitivity which reads as follows: *'The Press should be gender sensitive and avoid stereotyping when reporting.'*

A model: The Tanzania Media Gender Code of Ethics

Tanzania is one of the few countries of the continent which has deemed it necessary to have a specific gender code of ethics for journalism, which has been adopted by stakeholders in 2009. The Media Council of Tanzania thus has a Media Gender Code of Ethics which is meant to be read together with its Professional Code of Ethics for Journalists. This code starts by providing a useful definition of terms such as discrimination, gender stereotyping, negative gender portrayal and sexist language. The main sections cover the following:

- Accuracy and fairness: equal space for men and women, more gender specific coverage to challenge stereotypes, training for journalists and continuous learning on gender issues

- Balance, credibility and impartiality: diversity regardless of social standing, involvement of women in production of gender related programmes

- Accountability: holding all policy makers accountable for gender mainstreaming

- Gender stereotyping: avoiding identification of sexual violence, exploitation of women and children as helpless or deserving victims, degrading women, gender oppression and stereotyping, glamourising violence against women, depiction of sexual acts

- Language: use of sexist language, oversimplification, respect for dignity

- Marketing and advertising: gender stereotyping and negative portrayals

- Gender sensitivity within workplaces: gender balance in recruitment and selection policies, inclusive access to training and mentoring, sexual harassment policies, equal opportunities in allocation of news beats, career pathing and promotion.

Conclusion

Beyond the simplistic representation of gender wars as a simple women against men struggles reserved for hysterical moralising feminists or brainless sextremists, gender sensitive reporting is essential to contributing to a more balanced representation of society. Sane relations between different gender groups at all levels of society rest on a respectful and dignified representation of all actors as well as appropriate space for diverse voices.

This is why a Gender Code of Ethics for the Media is being proposed for adoption by all media houses either as part of their internal code of ethics or as part of the common code of ethics to be adopted by the industry as a whole.

A Gender Code of Ethics for the Media

Gender equality is an integral part of freedom of expression as all gender categories have the right to be heard and seen in the public sphere as full-fledge citizens participating in a democratic society. Gender balance is thus important in news reporting. Equally important is the need to challenge prevailing gender stereotypes.

Journalists endeavour to recognise the diversity of race, ethnicity, religion, sex, ability, sexuality, age and class. They shall strive to eliminate discrimination on the basis of gender from their respective publication and pledge to put more effort to provide for more balance, fairness and accuracy in their reports. They shall strive to be inclusive by seeking a diversity of voices rather than rely solely on usual male dominant sources.

Journalists and media houses shall NOT:

- use discriminatory or sexist language. In case they are citing such language as used by the subjects of their articles, they shall use appropriate quotation marks and reporting verbs while taking care not to promote or support the person quoted.

- depict women in general as inferior, secondary class citizens.

- resort to gender stereotyping of roles (e.g. loving, caring women, tough men, effeminate gays, masculinised lesbians, etc.).

- have recourse to the commoditisation of the female body and gratuitous sexualised and eroticised views of women who are portrayed in the news.

- pander to lurid curiosity.

- publish the identity (name, picture) of rape victims and victims of sexual violence and other sexual offences without informed consent. They shall take all precautions to protect the identity of such victims so that the latter are not subjected to stigmatisation and further trauma.

- glamourise violence against women and sexual minorities such as lesbians, gays, bisexuals, transgender (LGBT).

- advocate hatred based on gender, nor incite to cause harm.

- encourage misogyny and the reinforcement of patriarchy.

In the workplace, media houses shall allow journalists to work across a diversity of beats, irrespective of gender category. They shall ensure that selection, recruitment, career pathing, capacity building, training, fast tracking and promotion are devoid of gender discrimination and that there is no tolerance for sexual harassment in the workplace. They shall encourage friendly work practices and mutual respect between men and women. Media houses shall encourage the active pursuit of knowledge in gender issues and incorporate same in their training programmes. They shall develop policies to ensure gender balance in coverage and gender equality in the workplace.

This Gender Code of Ethics should be read in line with any General Code of Ethics, whether developed by media houses, media associations or regulators.

References

- Bennett, T, Curran, J., Gurevitch, M. Woollacott, J. (1982). *Culture, Society and the Media.* : Methuen & Co Ltd.

- Butler, J.. (1990). Gender Trouble: Feminism and the Subversion of Identity. : Routledge Classics.

- Certeau, M.. (1984). The Practice of Everyday Life.. : University of California Press.

- Fiske, J.. (1989). Understanding Popular Culture. : Routledge.

- Greer, G.. (1999). The Whole Woman. : Transworld Publishers Ltd.

- Hall, S. (1973). "Encoding and Decoding in the Television Discourse", Centre for Cultural Studies, University of Birmingham, CCS Stencilled Paper no. 7.

- IBA Code of Ethics

- IFJ. (2009). Rétablir l'équilibre: Égalité des genres dans le journalisme. / Gender equality in journalism : setting the balance right.

- La Sentinelle, Code de Déontologie des Journalistes - *http://www.lexpress.mu/code-de-deontologie*

- NEPA, Code de Pratiques Professionnelles de la Presse Mauricienne -*http://comstudies.files.wordpress.com/2012/10/code-de-pratiques-professionnelles-de-la-presse-mauricienne.pdf*

- Tuchman, G. (1978). The symbolic annihilation of women by the mass media, Oxford University Press

- UNESCO, Guidelines on Gender-Neutral Language, 1999

- US Department of Justice. (2004). Ethics of news media in covering cases of sexual crimes.

ADDENDA

Three basic documents govern the regulation of the print media in South Africa – the Press Council's Press Code, the Complaints Procedures and its Constitution. What follows is the complete text of each of these documents. The website is www.presscouncil.org. za.

The BCCSA has its own Code. I have summarised the parts of this Code that deals more specifically with ethical issues. Visit www. bccsa.co.za for the full text.

I believe that it is necessary to include these texts here, questions of regulation are still unresolved in Mauritius. These documents therefore serve as an example, which would hopefully be helpful to those who strive for independent and credible regulation in their country.

A.   The South African Press Council

1.   The Press Code

The Preamble

The press exists to serve society. Its freedom provides for independent scrutiny of the forces that shape society, and is essential to realising the promise of democracy. It enables citizens to make informed judgments on the issues of the day, a role whose centrality is recognised in the South African Constitution.

Section 16 of the Bill of Rights sets out that:

1. "Everyone has the right to freedom of expression, which includes:

a) Freedom of the press and other media;

b) Freedom to receive and impart information or ideas;

c) Freedom of artistic creativity; and

d) Academic freedom and freedom of scientific research.

2. "The right in subsection (1) does not extend to:

a) Propaganda for war;

b) Incitement of imminent violence; or

c) Advocacy of hatred that is based on race, ethnicity, gender or religion,

and that constitutes incitement to cause harm."

The press strives to hold these rights in trust for the country's citizens; and it is subject to the same rights and duties as the individual. Everyone has the duty to defend and further these rights, in recognition of the struggles that created them: the media, the public and government, who all make up the democratic state.

Our work is guided at all times by the public interest, understood to describe information of legitimate interest or importance to citizens.

As journalists, we commit ourselves to the highest standards of excellence, to maintain credibility and keep the trust of our readers. This means always striving for truth, avoiding unnecessary harm, reflecting a multiplicity of voices in our coverage of events, showing a special concern for children and other vulnerable groups, and acting independently.

We adopt the following Press Code:

The Press Code

1. Gathering of news

1.1. News should be obtained legally, honestly and fairly, unless public interest dictates otherwise.

1.2. Press representatives shall identify themselves as such, unless public interest or their safety dictates otherwise.

2. Reporting of News

2.1. The press shall take care to report news truthfully, accurately and fairly.

2.2. News shall be presented in context and in a balanced manner, without any intentional or negligent departure from the facts whether by distortion, exaggeration or misrepresentation, material omissions, or summarisation.

2.3. Only what may reasonably be true, having regard to the sources of the news, may be presented as fact, and such facts shall be published fairly with due regard to context and importance. Where a report is not based on facts or is founded on opinion, allegation, rumour or supposition, it shall be presented in such manner as to indicate this clearly.

2.4. Where there is reason to doubt the accuracy of a report and it is practicable to verify the accuracy thereof, it shall be verified. Where it has not been practicable to verify the accuracy of a report, this shall be stated in such report.

2.5. A publication shall seek the views of the subject of critical reportage in advance of publication; provided that this need not be done where the publication has reasonable grounds for believing that by doing so it would be prevented from publishing the report or where evidence might be destroyed or sources intimidated. Reasonable time should be afforded the subject for a response. If the publication is unable to obtain such comment, this shall be stated in the report.

2.6. A publication shall make amends for publishing information or comment that is found to be inaccurate by printing, promptly and with appropriate prominence, a retraction, correction or explanation.

2.7. Reports, photographs or sketches relating to indecency or obscenity shall be presented with due sensitivity to the prevailing moral climate. A visual presentation of explicit sex shall not be published, unless public interest dictates otherwise.

2.8. Journalists shall not plagiarise.

3. Independence and conflicts of interest

3.1 The press shall not allow commercial, political, personal or other non- professional considerations to influence or slant reporting. Conflicts of interest must be avoided, as well as arrangements or practices that could lead audiences to doubt the press's independence and professionalism.

3.2 Journalists shall not accept a bribe, gift or any other benefit where this is intended or likely to influence coverage.

3.3 The press shall indicate clearly when an outside organisation has contributed to the cost of newsgathering.

3.4 Editorial material shall be kept clearly distinct from advertising.

4. Dignity, Reputation and Privacy

4.1. The press shall exercise care and consideration in matters involving the private lives and concerns of individuals. The right to privacy may be overridden by a legitimate public interest.

4.2. The press shall exercise care and consideration in matters involving dignity and reputation. The dignity or reputation of an individual should only be overridden in the following circumstances:

4.2.1. The facts reported are true or substantially true;

4.2.2. The article amounts to fair comment based on facts that are adequately referred to and that are true or substantially true;

4.2.3. The report amounts to a fair and accurate report of court proceedings, Parliamentary proceedings or the proceedings of any quasi-judicial tribunal or forum; or

4.2.4. It was reasonable for the article to be published because it was prepared in accordance with acceptable principles of journalistic conduct and in the public interest.

4.3. The identity of rape victims and victims of sexual violence shall not be published without the consent of the victim or in the case of children, without the consent of their legal guardians and it is in the best interest of the child.

4.4. The HIV/AIDS status of people should not be disclosed without their consent, or in the case of children, without the consent of their legal guardians, and only if it is in the public interest and it is in the best interest of the child.

5. Discrimination and Hate Speech

5.1. Except where it is strictly relevant to the matter reported and it is in the public interest to do so, the press shall avoid discriminatory or denigratory references to people's race, gender, sex, pregnancy, marital status, ethnic or social origin, colour, sexual orientation, age, disability, religion, conscience, belief, culture, language and birth or other status, nor shall it refer to people's status in a prejudicial or pejorative context.

5.2. The press has the right and indeed the duty to report and comment on all matters of legitimate public interest. This right and duty must, however, be balanced against the obligation not to publish material that amounts to:

5.2.1. Propaganda for war;

5.2.2. Incitement of imminent violence; or

5.2.3. Advocacy of hatred that is based on race, ethnicity, gender or religion, and that constitutes incitement to cause harm.

6. Advocacy

A publication is justified in strongly advocating its own views on controversial topics provided that it treats its readers fairly by:

6.1. Making fact and opinion clearly distinguishable;

6.2. Not misrepresenting or suppressing relevant facts; and

6.3. Not distorting the facts.

7. Comment

7.1. The press shall be entitled to comment upon or criticise any actions or events of public interest provided such comments or criticisms are fairly and honestly made.

7.2. Comment by the press shall be presented in such manner that it appears clearly that it is comment, and shall be made on facts truly stated or fairly indicated and referred to.

7.3. Comment by the press shall be an honest expression of opinion, without malice or dishonest motives, and shall take fair account of all available facts which are material to the matter commented upon.

8. Children

The Bill of Rights (Section 28.2) in the South African Constitution states: "A child's best interests are of paramount importance in every matter concerning the child."

8.1. The press shall therefore exercise exceptional care and consideration when reporting about children under the age of 18. If there is any chance that coverage might cause harm of any kind to a child, he or she shall not be interviewed, photographed or identified unless a custodial parent or similarly responsible adult consents, or a public interest is evident.

8.2. Child pornography shall not be published.

Child Pornography is defined in the Film and Publications Act as: Any image or any description of a person, real or simulated, who is or who is depicted or described as being, under the age of 18 years, engaged in sexual conduct; participating in or assisting another person to participate in sexual conduct; or showing or describing the body or parts of the body of the person in a manner or parts of the body of the person in a manner or circumstance which, in context, amounts to sexual exploitation.

8.3. The press shall not identify children who have been victims of abuse, exploitation, or who have been charged with or convicted of a crime, unless a public interest is evident and it is in the best interests of the child.

9. Violence

Due care and responsibility shall be exercised by the press with regard to the presentation of brutality, violence and suffering.

10. Headlines, Posters, Pictures and Captions

10.1. Headlines and captions to pictures shall give a reasonable reflection of the contents of the report or picture in question.

10.2. Posters shall not mislead the public and shall give a reasonable reflection of the contents of the reports in question.

10.3. Pictures shall not misrepresent or mislead nor be manipulated to do so.

11. Confidential and anonymous sources

11.1. The press has an obligation to protect confidential sources of information.

11.2. The press shall avoid the use of anonymous sources unless there is no other way to deal with a story. Care should be taken to corroborate the information.

11.3. The press shall not publish information that constitutes a breach of confidence, unless a legitimate public interest dictates otherwise.

12. Payment for Articles

The press shall avoid shady journalism in which informants are paid to induce them to give the information, particularly when they are criminals - except where the material concerned ought to be published in the public interest and the payment is necessary for this to be done.

2.   Complaints Procedures

It shall be of the essence of the mediation and adjudication proceedings that:

- Complaints be considered and mediated or adjudicated on within the shortest possible time after the publication of the matter giving rise to the complaint;

- Complaints be considered and mediated or adjudicated in an informal manner.

1. Complaints

1.1. "Complainant" shall mean and include any person who or body of persons which lodges a complaint and has standing to complain in terms of the following rule: anyone acting in their own interest; anyone acting on behalf of another person who cannot act in his or her own name; anyone acting as a member of, or in the interest of, a group or class of persons; and an association acting in the interest of its members.

1.2. The "respondent" in respect of a complaint shall be the proprietor of the publication, which shall delegate its editor or, in his or her absence, an assistant editor or other suitable editorial representative of the member concerned, to act and appear in its stead in respect of any complaints dealt with by the Public Advocate, the Ombudsman or the Chair of Appeals.

1.3. A complaint shall be made as soon as possible, but not later than 20 working days after the date of publication giving rise to the complaint. The Public Advocate, who throughout the entire process (also at the Ombudsman and the Appeals Panel) will advise and assist the complainant if the complainant agrees, may on reasonable grounds accept late complaints if, in his or her opinion, there is a good and satisfactory explanation for the delay.

1.4. The complaint shall be made to the Public Advocate either in person, by telephone or in writing. "Writing" shall include cable, telegram, telex, SMS, e-mail and fax messages. Where a complaint is made other than in writing it shall be confirmed forthwith in writing or the Public Advocate's office shall assist the complainant to do so before the complaint can be formally accepted. On receipt of a complaint, the Public Advocate shall be entitled to request from the complainant a copy of the material published giving rise to the complaint, and the complainant shall be obliged to forward such a copy to the Public Advocate forthwith.

1.5. The Public Advocate shall not accept a complaint:

1.5.1. Which is anonymous; or

1.5.2. Which, in his or her opinion, is fraudulent, frivolous, malicious or vexatious or *prima facie* falls outside the ambit of the Press Code; or

1.5.3. Which is directed at a newspaper outside the jurisdiction of the Ombudsman. Where a publication does not fall within the jurisdiction of the Ombudsman, the Public Advocate will approach the proprietor or editor of the publication and request that the publication submits to the process for purposes of adjudicating the complaint.

1.6. Where at any stage of the proceedings it emerges that proceedings before a court are pending on a matter related to the material complained about, the Public Advocate, the

Ombudsman or the Chair of Appeals, depending on status of the complaint at that stage, shall forthwith stop the proceedings and set aside the acceptance of the complaint by the Public Advocate.

1.7. Where the Public Advocate declines to accept a complaint on any of the grounds specified in rule 1.5 the complainant may, within seven working days, with full reasons, request the Ombudsman to adjudicate the complaint in terms of Section 3. The Deputy Ombudsman or another competent member of the Panel of Adjudicators may act on behalf of the complainant as the Public Advocate in this event. Either party may take the Ombudsman's or the Adjudicating Panel's ruling to the Chair of Appeals in terms of normal procedures.

1.8. Where, within 30 working days after the date of publication there has been no complaint, but the Public Advocate is of the view that a prima facie contravention of the Press Code has been committed and it is in the public interest, he may file a complaint with the Ombudsman for adjudication in terms of Section 3 below.

2. Settlement procedure by the Public Advocate

2.1. Upon formal acceptance of a complaint by the Public Advocate he or she shall immediately notify the publication of the complaint in writing, giving sufficient details to enable the respondent to investigate the matter and respond within seven working days unless a satisfactory reason is given to the Public Advocate for an extension of time.

2.2. The Public Advocate shall forthwith endeavour with the complainant to achieve a speedy settlement with the publication.

2.3. If the complaint is not settled within 15 working days of the publication receiving notice of the complaint, the Public

Advocate shall refer the complaint to the Ombudsman for adjudication, unless she or he feels the time-frame needs to be lengthened because of the circumstances.

3. Adjudication by the Ombudsman

3.1. The Ombudsman may, if it is reasonable not to hear the parties, decide the matter on the papers.

3.2. If the Ombudsman finds that the matter cannot be decided on the papers, but some aspects of a complaint need to be clarified and sees no need for a formal hearing, the Ombudsman may convene an informal hearing with the two parties.

3.3. Where the Ombudsman decides to hold a hearing, he or she shall convene an Adjudication Panel in which the Ombudsman is joined by a public and a press member drawn from the Panel of Adjudicators, to adjudicate the matter with him or her at a hearing.

3.3.1. A person employed by a publication which is the subject of the complaint, or with any other vested interest in the matter, may not serve on an Adjudication Panel to consider the matter.

3.4. Both parties are expected to attend and address the Adjudication Panel, which is, in any case, entitled to question them personally or in writing on the matter. Failure by the publication to send a representative may lead to the matter being adjudicated in their absence.

3.5. Decisions by the Adjudication Panel shall be by a majority vote.

3.6. Within 7 working days of receipt of the decision, any one of the parties may apply for leave to appeal to the Chair of Appeals and the grounds of appeal shall be fully set out.

3.7. The application and grounds must be filed at the Ombudsman's office.

3.8. The Ombudsman shall inform the other party of the application for leave to appeal and shall advise the party that he or she may file a response to the application for leave to appeal within 7 working days of receipt thereof.

3.9. If the Chair of Appeals is of the view that there are reasonable prospects that the Appeals Panel may come to a decision different from that of the Ombudsman or the Adjudications Panel, as the case may be, the Chair of Appeals shall grant leave to appeal.

4. Adjudication by the Appeals Committee

4.1. Where leave to appeal is granted in terms of rule 3.7, the Ombudsman shall place before the Chair of Appeals all the documentation that he or she had before him or her.

4.2. The Chair of Appeals shall appoint one press member and up to three public members from the Panel of Adjudicators appointed in terms of clause 5.6 of the Constitution, to hear the appeal with him or her. The Chair of Appeals will have discretion on the number of public members he or she invites to hear an appeal with him.

4.2.1. A person employed by a publication which is the subject of the complaint, or with any other vested interest in the matter, may not serve on an Appeals Panel to consider the matter.

4.2.2. Members of the Panel of Adjudicators who heard a case with the Ombudsman may not be part of a panel hearing the appeal against the earlier decision.

4.3. The Chair of Appeals shall determine a date, time and venue for adjudication of the appeal, which shall be heard as soon as possible after receipt by him or her of the documents referred to in rule 4.1.

4.4. The Ombudsman shall inform the parties of the date and venue of the hearing before the Appeals Panel.

4.5. Both parties are expected to attend and address the Appeals Panel, which is, in any case, entitled to question them personally or in writing on the matter. Failure by the publication to send a representative may lead to the matter being adjudicated in their absence.

5. Hearings

5.1. Discussions between the Public Advocate and the complainant, on the one hand, and the publication, on the other, are private and confidential and are conducted on a without prejudice basis. No person may refer to anything said at these discussions, during any subsequent proceedings, unless the parties agree in writing. No person may be called as a witness during any subsequent proceedings in the Press Council or in any court to give evidence about what transpired during the discussions.

5.2. The hearings of the Adjudicating Panel and of the Appeals Panel shall be open to the public unless the identity of a rape victim or victim of a sexual offence, a child under eighteen, or a victim of extortion is at issue.

5.3. The Public Advocate may assist the complainant at a hearing of the Adjudicating Panel or the Appeals Panel.

5.4. Legal representation shall not be permitted at hearings unless:

5.4.1. The Ombudsman or the Chair of Appeals and all the other parties consent;

5.4.2. The Ombudsman or the Chair of Appeals concludes that it is unreasonable to expect a party to deal with the dispute without legal representation, after considering:

5.4.2.1. The nature of the questions of law raised by the dispute;

5.4.2.2. The complexity of the dispute;

5.4.2.3. The public interest; and

5.4.2.4. The comparative ability of the opposing parties to deal with the dispute.

5.5. At the conclusion of a hearing, and before a Panel has reached a decision, both parties shall be entitled to address the Panel, personally or in writing, on sanctions and where appropriate mitigation.

6. Variation of Procedure

6.1. The Ombudsman or Chair of Appeals may, depending at which level the matter is being adjudicated, if satisfied that no injustice will result, and upon such conditions as he or she may impose:

6.1.1. Extend any time period contemplated in these rules;

6.1.2. At any stage require any allegation of fact to be verified on oath; and

6.1.3. Call on the parties to a dispute to furnish such further information as he or she may consider necessary.

7. Findings of the Ombudsman, Adjudication Panel, the Chair of Appeals and the Appeals Panel

7.1. The Ombudsman, the Adjudication Panel, the Chair of Appeals and the Appeals Panel may uphold or dismiss a complaint or appeal, as the case may be. Such finding must be handed down within 21 days of the hearing of the complaint.

7.2. If a finding is made against a member of PMSA or a publication that has voluntarily become subject to the jurisdiction of the Ombudsman, the Ombudsman, the Adjudication Panel, or the Appeals Panel, as the case may be, may make any one or more of the following orders against the proprietor of the publication:

7.2.1. Caution or reprimand the publication;

7.2.2. Direct that a correction, retraction or explanation and, where appropriate, an apology and/or the findings of the Ombudsman, the Adjudication Panel, or the Appeals Panel be published by the respondent in such manner as they may determine.

7.2.3. Order that a complainant's reply to a published article, comment or letter be published by the publication;

7.2.4. Make any supplementary or ancillary orders or issue directives that are considered necessary for carrying into effect the orders or directives made in terms of this clause and, more particularly, issue directives as to the publication of the findings of the Ombudsman, the Adjudication Panel, or the Appeals Panel.

8. Hierarchy of sanctions

8.1. A hierarchy of sanctions must be developed by the Press Council according to a scale of seriousness of infractions and, when that is done, this hierarchy must be included i n this sub-clause and taken into consideration in determining a fitting sanction in terms of this clause.

8.2. "Space fines" shall be applied by way of the amount of space imposed to be correspondent with the seriousness of the infraction.

8.3. Monetary fines will not be imposed as a penalty for the content of the press.

However, monetary fines according to a formula determined by the Press Council and included in this sub-clause and/or suspension for a period or expulsion from the jurisdiction of the Ombudsman may be imposed as sanctions for a respondent's failure to appear for adjudication hearings and repeated non-compliance with the rulings of the adjudicatory system.

9. Records

9.1 The Ombudsman shall cause any findings, and reasons for a finding to be sent to the complainant and to the respondent who shall comply with the Press Ombudsman Panel or the Press Appeals Panel's orders or directives, if any.

9.2 The Ombudsman shall keep on record all findings and reasons for findings by the Press Ombudsman Panel or the Press Appeals Panel.

9.3 The records referred to in rule 9.1 shall be public documents except insofar as those documents identify a rape victim, a person who has been a victim of a sexual offence or a child under eighteen, or a victim of extortion or identify any other person whose identity is protected in the Press Code or by law.

3.   The Constitution

Preamble

- Reaffirming that the Bill of Rights, which includes freedom of expression, which in turn includes freedom of the press, is a cornerstone of democracy;

- Acknowledging that the South African Constitution guarantees freedom of expression and that South Africa is also party to the 2002 Declaration of Principles on Freedom of Expression in Africa, drawn up by the African Commission on Human and Peoples' Rights, which states: "Effective self-regulation is the best system for promoting high standards in the media";

- Believing that the effectiveness of self-regulation by the print media is enhanced by public participation in a co-regulatory process;

- Noting that the laws of the country allow for alternative dispute resolution through a speedy and cost-effective process; and

- Accepting that co-regulation involving exclusively the press and the public will uphold freedom of expression and the editorial independence of the press, and contribute to high standards of journalism and ethical conduct.

We, the print media in South Africa, therefore establish a voluntary independent

co-regulatory system involving exclusively representatives of the press and representatives of the public with the aims and objectives set out in this Constitution.

1. Establishment of the Press Council of South Africa

1.1. The South African Press, through the founding industry and professional bodies named in paragraph 1.2, establishes the Press Council of South Africa ("PCSA" or "Council"), in order to achieve the aims and objectives set out in paragraph 2 of this Constitution.

1.2. The founding associations are:

1.2.1. Print Media South Africa (PMSA), which includes:

1.2.1.1. The Newspaper Association of South Africa (NASA);

1.2.1.2. The Magazine Publishers Association of South Africa (MPASA);

1.2.1.3. The Association of Independent Publishers (AIP);

1.2.2. The Forum of Community Journalists (FCJ); and

1.2.3. The South African National Editors' Forum (SANEF), which also acts in trust for a journalists' association until such an association is formed.

1.3. The constituent associations named in 1.2 explicitly guarantee the independence of the PCSA, so that it can act without fear or favour in the interests of a free and ethical press, and in pursuit of the aims and objectives set out below.

2. Aims and Objectives

2.1. To promote and to develop ethical practice in journalism and to promote the adoption of and adherence to those standards by the South African press;

2.2. To adopt the SA Press Code as a guide to excellent practice, and to act as its custodian;

2.3. To establish and maintain a voluntary independent mechanism to deal with complaints about journalistic ethics from the public against member publications of PMSA and others who subscribe to the SA Press Code;

2.4. To promote and preserve the right of freedom of expression, including freedom of the press as guaranteed in Section 16 of the Constitution of the Republic of South Africa;

2.5. To promote the concept of independent press co-regulation involving exclusively representatives of the press and representatives of the public, as well as public awareness of the existence of the PCSA's mediation and adjudication services to deal with complaints about journalistic practice;

2.6. To cooperate with other press councils and similar organisations in South Africa and abroad that have the same aims and objectives as the PCSA; and

2.7. To undertake such other tasks as are necessary to further the objectives of the Council.

3. Powers and functions

3.1. The Council shall have the power to consider and decide on any matter arising from this Constitution or the functioning of any office appointed in terms of this Constitution;

3.2. The Council shall perform all such acts and do all such things as are reasonably necessary for or ancillary, incidental or supplementary to the achievement, pursuit, furtherance or promotion of the objects and principles contained in this Constitution, the Press Code, Complaints Procedure or any function considered necessary by the Council; and

3.3. The PCSA may set up a management committee and/ or other sub-committees to deal with particular issues, as it sees fit.

4. Composition of Council

4.1. The Council shall consist of a retired judge and 12 individuals representing members of the public and members of the media. The judge shall hold no other position in the Press Council or its appeals mechanism.

4.2. The outgoing PCSA shall request the Chief Justice of South Africa to recommend a judge who is no longer in active service to chair the Press Council.

4.3. Six of the representatives shall be appointed by the Appointments Panel, as set out in 5.2. of this constitution, from nominations received from members of the public.

4.4. Six of the representatives shall be from the press and shall be appointed by the constituent associations as follows:

4.4.1. One member by the Newspaper Association of South Africa (NASA);

4.4.2. One member by the Magazine Publishers Association of South Africa (MPASA);

4.4.3.One member by the Association of Independent Publishers (AIP); and

4.4.4. One member by the Forum of Community Journalists (FCJ).

4.4.5.The South African National Editors' Forum (SANEF) shall appoint two members, and in the event of a journalists' association being formed, SANEF shall relinquish one seat to the journalists' association.

4.5. In the appointments, the Appointments Panel and the constituent associations should strive to reflect the diversity of the people of South Africa.

4.6. After its appointment, the Council shall elect from among the members of Council a Deputy Chairperson, provided that in the event the deputy in one term is a public representative, the deputy in the following term will be a press representative, and vice versa.

4.7. The members of the Council shall serve for five years, but are eligible to re-apply for the positions at the end of the term. However, to ensure the necessary continuity, three press and three public members shall be appointed for two and a half years for the first term of appointment after this amended Constitution becomes operational. Thereafter, all the terms will revert to overlapping five years. At its first regular meeting, the first Council shall decide who shall serve for two and a half years and who shall serve for five years.

4.8. In the event of a press vacancy occurring, the organisation whose representative has left shall appoint a replacement for the balance of the term.

4.9. In the event of a public vacancy occurring, the Appointments Panel shall appoint a replacement, preferably from the shortlist of candidates previously considered.

4.10. The Director, Press Ombudsman and Public Advocate

appointed in terms of 5.2.2 below shall serve ex-officio on the PCSA, without voting rights.

5. Structures and officers of the Council

The PCSA shall establish and maintain the following structures:

5.1. Complaints mechanism

5.1.1. The PCSA shall establish a mechanism to deal with complaints against the press. The mechanism – made up of the Public Advocate, the Press Ombudsman and their deputies, the Panel of Adjudicators and the Chair of Appeals, as enumerated below in this Constitution – offers a non-statutory avenue for the mediation and adjudication of complaints against the press. The offices and structures dealing with complaints shall act independently of the PCSA and the constituent media organisations.

5.1.2. The member publications of the associations listed in paragraph 1.2. above are subject to the Press Code, as amended from time to time by the PCSA, and to the jurisdiction of the PCSA's complaints mechanism.

5.1.3. The jurisdiction of the PCSA extends to the electronic media of member publications.

5.1.4. Where a complaint is made against a newspaper or magazine which is not a member of the associations listed in paragraph 1.2. above, the Public Advocate or Ombudsman shall approach such newspaper or magazine to establish whether it accepts the jurisdiction of the PCSA.

5.1.5. In the event that the newspaper or magazine refuses to submit to the jurisdiction of the Ombudsman, the Public Advocate or Ombudsman shall advise the complainant accordingly.

5.2. Appointments Panel

5.2.1. The PCSA shall request the Chief Justice of South

Africa to recommend a judge who is no longer in active service to chair the Appointments Panel.

5.2.2. The Appointments Panel shall be responsible for the appointment of public members of the PCSA, the public members of the Panel of Adjudicators, the Ombudsman, the Director, the Public Advocate and any deputies for these officers when necessary.

5.2.3. These appointees:

5.2.3.1. Shall be citizens of and permanently resident in the Republic of South Africa;

5.2.3.2. Shall be committed to the values underpinning the South African Constitution, as well as to the Press Code of the PCSA; and

5.2.3.3. Shall be of high standing and integrity.

5.2.4. The sitting Council shall appoint up to four Council members, preferably consisting of two press and two public representatives, to assist the Chairperson of the Appointments Panel.

5.2.5. All appointments of the public members of the PCSA and the public members of the Panel of Adjudicators shall be made after invitations to the public for nomination have been advertised, a shortlist compiled and interviews conducted with shortlisted candidates.

5.2.6. The Director, the Ombudsman, and the Public Advocate will be appointed by the Panel after the positions have been widely advertised and it has interviewed shortlisted candidates.

5.2.7. The Appointments Panel will dissolve when it has completed its task but will be prepared to reconvene to deal with any vacancies that may arise.

5.2.8. In the event of a vacancy occurring for any reason,

the Appointments Panel shall be requested to reconvene to appoint a replacement for the balance of the term, preferably from previously shortlisted candidates.

5.3. The Director

5.3.1. The Director shall lead the PCSA on a full-time, professional basis and will concentrate on public engagement regarding issues of ethical journalism and media freedom.

5.3.2. The Director shall serve a renewable term of five years.

5.4. The Ombudsman

5.4.1. The references to the Ombudsman in this section apply to the Deputy Ombudsman as well when he deputises for the Ombudsman.

5.4.2. The Ombudsman's term of office is five years, which may be renewed.

5.4.3. The Ombudsman shall adjudicate matters that cannot be resolved at the earlier level of mediation.

5.4.4. The Ombudsman may do so on the papers, without hearing evidence.

5.4.5 The Ombudsman may also conduct a hearing, for which the Ombudsman shall convene an Adjudication Panel, in which s/he shall be joined by one press and one public member of the Panel of Adjudicators.

5.4.6. The Ombudsman may also co-opt an assessor without voting rights to assist the Adjudication Panel with technically complex issues.

5.5. Public Advocate

5.5.1 The Public Advocate should ideally have media skills and understand the workings of the South African legal system, and have a finely tuned sense of public service and commitment.

5.5.2 The Public Advocate may serve a renewable term of five years.

5.5.3 The Public Advocate shall assist members of the public to formulate their complaints, attempt to resolve complaints amicably by liaising directly with the publication on behalf of the complainant.

5.5.4. Where the Public Advocate does not succeed in having a complaint settled within 15 working days after the complaint was lodged with a publication, he or she shall refer the unresolved dispute to the Ombudsman for adjudication as per the Complaints Procedures.

5.5.5. The Public Advocate may represent the complainant before the Ombudsman and/or the Appeals Panel.

5.6. The Panel of Adjudicators

5.6.1. The Panel of Adjudicators shall consist of eight public representatives and six press representatives, none of whom shall be members of the Council.

5.6.2. The Appointments Panel shall appoint the eight public members of the Panel of Adjudicators and the constituent associations listed in 1.2 of this constitution shall appoint the press representatives.

5.6.3. Members of the Adjudication Panel who hear a case with the Ombudsman shall be drawn from the Panel of Adjudicators, as set out in paragraph 5.4.5 above.

5.6.4. The members of the Panel of Adjudicators shall serve for five years, but are eligible to re-apply for the positions at the end of the term. However, to ensure the necessary continuity three press and four public members shall be appointed for two and a half years for the first term of appointment after this amended Constitution becomes operational. Thereafter, all the terms will revert to overlapping five years. When the

Panel of Adjudicators first convenes, the meeting shall decide who shall serve for two and a half years and who shall serve for five years.

5.7. The Chair of Appeals

5.7.1. The Chair of Appeals shall be a senior legal practitioner, preferably a retired judge, appointed by the Council on the recommendation of the Chief Justice and may be the same judge who chairs the Appointments Panel.

5.7.2. The Chair of Appeals shall deal with appeals against a ruling by the Ombudsman, acting with or without an Adjudication Panel.

5.7.3. Application for leave to appeal must be made to the Chair of Appeals, who may accept the application or refuse it.

5.7.4. The Chair of Appeals may also convene an Appeals Panel, in which the Chair of Appeals shall be joined by one press and up to three public members of the Adjudication Panel. The Chair of Appeals will have discretion on the number of public members to hear an appeal. Decisions of the Appeal Panel shall be by majority vote.

5.7.5. A person employed by a publication which is the subject of the complaint, or with any other vested interest in the matter, may not serve on an Appeals Panel to consider the matter.

5.7.6. The Appeals Panel may consider the matter with or without hearing oral argument or evidence.

5.7.7. The term of appointment of the Chair of Appeals shall be for five years and is part-time.

5.7.8. The Chair of Appeals shall depute a member of the Panel of Adjudicators to act as chairperson when the Chair of Appeals is not available.

6. Eligibility for membership of Council and of the Panel of Adjudicators

6.1. Members appointed to the Council must be persons who:

6.1.1. Are of high standing and integrity with a strong interest in the press, subscribe fully to the principles of a free press and the Press Code and who shall act in the furtherance of the aims and objectives of the Council; and

6.1.2. Shall be committed to the values underpinning the SA Constitution, as well as to the Press Code of the PCSA.

6.1.3. Are press members of the PCSA and who are required to be working journalists at one of the constituent associations or have wide experience in this field.

6.1.4. The public members of the Council and the Panel of Adjudicators are required to have a keen sense of fairness and balance, and the skills to apply their minds to issues in the press. In addition, they are required to have a keen interest in communications, media and in social and political issues, and be advocates of freedom of expression and freedom of the press, but may not be in the employ of the press.

6.1.5. The press members of the Panel of Adjudicators must have extensive knowledge of the press and its workings and shall be former or current senior journalists.

6.1.6. The following persons may not be appointed to any position on the PCSA or the Panel of Adjudicators:

6.1.6.1. Persons under the age of 21;

6.1.6.2. Any person who is not legally able to manage his or her own affairs;

6.1.6.3. Any person who is disqualified from being or remaining a director in terms of any legislation with respect to the formation and management of companies;

6.1.6.4. Any person who has any financial interest in the media;

6.1.6.5. Any person who occupies a seat in a local, provincial or national legislative body;

6.1.6.6. Any person who is an office-bearer of a political party or movement or is in the employ of the public service;

6.1.6.7. Any person who is an un-rehabilitated insolvent; and

6.1.6.8. Any person who was convicted of an offence after April 1994, whether in South Africa or elsewhere, for which such person has been sentenced to imprisonment without the option of a fine.

7. Cessation of membership

7.1. A person shall cease to occupy an office of the PCSA or the Panel of Adjudicators if:

7.1.1. He or she resigns;

7.1.2. He or she becomes incapable for whatever reason of fulfilling his or her duties, provided that if a dispute arises between the incumbent and the PCSA in this connection, the matter will be resolved by an arbitrator appointed by the Chair of the Johannesburg Bar Council in a manner which he or she deems fair; or

7.1.3. He or she is declared insolvent by a court or is found guilty of an offence listed in Schedule I or II of the Criminal Procedure Act 1977.

7.2. Any member who becomes ineligible to hold the post in terms of the criteria for appointment to the post shall automatically cease to be a member as from the date of such ineligibility.

7.3. The Council may, by a two-thirds majority at a general meeting, suspend or terminate the membership of any member if such a member has brought the good name of the PCSA into disrepute or if such member has omitted to attend two consecutive meetings in a year without good cause acceptable to the Council.

7.4. Such a resolution must be taken by a two-thirds majority of all the members of the Council and may be taken only at a meeting where at least two-thirds of the members are in attendance.

7.5. At least 21 days' prior written notice of such a meeting of the Council must be given to all members of the Council.

8. Finance

8.1. The Council shall establish a Finance and Remuneration Committee to consider all financial issues and the fair and proper remuneration of its staff and the remuneration of public members. The Director of the PCSA shall be a member of this Committee.

8.2. The Finance and Remuneration Committee shall prepare an Annual Budget for submission to the PMSA.

8.3. The PMSA shall cover the reasonable costs of the PCSA.

8.4. If the PCSA and the PMSA cannot reach agreement on the annual budget, it shall be treated as a dispute and dealt with in terms of Section 11 of this Constitution.

8.5. The Chair of Appeals will be remunerated by way of a retainer, a daily hearing fee plus costs.

8.6. Public members of the Council will be remunerated per meeting and their costs for attending meetings will be paid by the PCSA.

8.7. The remuneration for the public members and the Chair of Appeals shall be determined by the PCSA at the beginning of its term and an annual increase of at least the official inflation rate (CPIX) shall also be determined at this stage.

8.8. Where members of the Panel of Adjudicators serve on an Adjudication Panel or an Appeals Panel, their costs and a reasonable daily rate for attendance shall be paid by the PCSA.

9. Meetings

9.1. The Council shall hold as many meetings per year as the Chairperson deems necessary, with a minimum of four meetings per year, or where three members require the Chairperson to hold a meeting on a specific matter, he or she shall do so within 21 days.

9.2. The quorum for a meeting shall be six members and resolutions shall be taken by majority vote except in so far as this Constitution requires otherwise. The Chairperson shall have a casting vote where the votes are equal.

9.3. Meetings of the Council may be held in person or by telephone or video conference or other appropriate electronic communications system or a combination thereof – provided that proper notice of such a meeting was given to all members and a quorum is in attendance.

9.4. Minutes shall be kept of the proceedings of meetings.

9.5. Unless all the members agree otherwise, a Council meeting shall be held within seven days' written notice by the Chairperson.

10. Amendments

10.1. Any amendment to this Constitution, the Code or the Complaints Procedure shall require the approval of two-thirds of the members of the Council voting either personally or in absentia, with the concurrence of the constituent associations.

10.2. No amendment shall be effective unless at least 21 calendar days written notice of a proposed amendment shall have been given to all members.

10.3. Votes submitted in absentia shall be in writing, signed by the relevant member and be recorded for or against the proposed amendment and no further amendments of the proposal may be made at such meeting unless a two-thirds majority of the Council is present at the meeting and votes for such further amendment.

11. Arbitration

11.1. In the event of any dispute within the PCSA or between the PCSA and its founding associations which are not capable of resolution between the parties within a period of two months, the PCSA and the associations shall appoint an arbitrator to resolve the problem and where the parties cannot agree on the arbitrator the Chair of the Johannesburg Bar Council shall be approached to appoint an arbitrator.

11.2. Each association which has appointed a representative in terms of 4.2 of this

Constitution shall bear the costs of its representative carrying out the bona fide functions.

11.3. The cost of the arbitrator shall be shared equally by the disputing parties except in the case where the arbitrator decides otherwise.

11.4. The decision of the arbitrator shall be final and binding.

12. Seat of the PCSA

12.1. The seat of the PCSA shall be in Johannesburg

and meetings shall be held in Johannesburg unless the management decides otherwise.

13. Dissolution

13.1. A resolution to dissolve the PCSA can only be passed at a special meeting called for this purpose, by a two-thirds majority of the members present, which two-thirds majority shall be not less than a simple majority of the total membership.

13.2. Not less than 21 days' notice shall be given of any such meeting and such notice shall give particulars of the purpose for which the meeting is called.

13.3. In the case of dissolution the assets will be handed back to the constituent associations.

B.   Summary of the BCCSA'S CODE

I have summarised the most important parts of this Code with regards to media ethics. You will see that the content of the Press Council's Code and that of the BCCSA is essentially the same.

Preamble

Freedom of expression lies at the foundation of a democratic South Africa and is one of the basic pre-requisites for this country's progress and the development in liberty of every person. Freedom of expression is a condition indispensable to the attainment of all other freedoms. The premium our Constitution attaches to freedom of expression is not novel, it is an article of faith, in the democracies of the kind we are venturing to create.

Constitutional protection is afforded to freedom of expression in Section 16 of the Constitution (see the preamble to the Press Code).

The outcome of disputes turning on the guarantee of freedom of expression will depend upon the value the courts are prepared to place on that freedom and the extent to which they will be inclined to subordinate other rights and interests to free expression. Rights of free expression will have to be weighed up against many other rights, including the rights to equality, dignity, privacy, political campaigning, fair trial, economic activity, workplace democracy, property and most significantly the rights of children and women.

In the period prior to the transition to democracy, governmental processes neither required nor welcomed the adjuncts of free expression and critical discussion and our country did not treasure at its core a democratic ideal. The right to freedom of expression was regularly violated with impunity by the legislature and the executive. Therefore the protection of this right is of paramount importance now that South Africa is grappling with the process of purging itself of those laws and practices from our past which do not accord with the values which underpin the Constitution.

Here are some sections in the Code:

News

Broadcasting service Licensees must report news truthfully, accurately and fairly.

News must be presented in the correct context and in a fair manner, without intentional or negligent departure from the facts, whether by distortion, exaggeration or misrepresentation, material omissions or summarisation.

Only that which may reasonably be true, having reasonable regard to the source of the news, may be presented as fact, and such fact must be broadcast fairly with reasonable regard to context and importance.

Where a report is not based on fact or is founded on opinion, supposition, rumours or allegations, it must be presented in such manner as to indicate, clearly that such is the case.

Where there is reason to doubt the correctness of the report and it is practicable to verify the correctness thereof, it must be verified. Where such verification is not practicable, that fact must be mentioned in the report.

Where it subsequently appears that a broadcast was incorrect in a material aspect, it must be rectified forthwith, without reservation or delay. The rectification must be presented with such a degree of prominence and timing as in the circumstances may be adequate and fair so as to readily attract attention.

The identity of rape victims and other victims of sexual violence must not be divulged in any broadcast, whether as part of news or not, without the prior valid consent of the victim concerned.

Broadcasting service licensees must advise viewers in advance of scenes or reporting of extraordinary violence, or graphic reporting on delicate subject-matter such as sexual assault or court action related to sexual crimes, particularly during afternoon or early evening newscasts and updates.

Broadcasting service licensees must not include explicit or graphic language related to news of destruction, accidents or sexual violence which could disturb children or sensitive audiences, except where it is in the public interest to include such material.

Comment

Broadcasting service licensees are entitled to broadcast comment on and criticism of any actions or events of public importance.

Comment must be an honest expression of opinion and must be presented in such manner that it appears clearly to be comment, and must be made on facts truly stated or fairly indicated and referred to.

Where a person has stated that he or she is not available for comment or such a person could not reasonably be reached, it must be stated in the programme.

Controversial Issues of Public Importance

In presenting a programme in which a controversial issue of public importance is discussed, a broadcaster must make reasonable efforts to fairly present opposing points of view either in the same programme or in a subsequent programme forming part of the same series of programmes presented within reasonable period of time of the original broadcast and within substantially the same time slot.

A person whose views are to be criticised in a broadcasting programme on a controversial issue of public importance must be given the right to reply to such criticism on the same programme. If this is impracticable, reasonable opportunity to respond to the programme should be provide where appropriate, for examples in a right to reply programme or in a pre-arranged discussion programme with the prior consent of the person concerned.

Privacy, Dignity and Reputation

Broadcasting service licensees must exercise exceptional care and consideration in matters involving the privacy, dignity and reputation of individuals, bearing in mind that the said rights may be overridden by a legitimate public interest.

In the protection of privacy, dignity and reputation special weight must be afforded to South African cultural customs concerning the privacy and dignity of people who are bereaved and their respect for those who have passed away.

In the protection of privacy, dignity and reputation special weight must be afforded to the privacy, dignity and reputation of children, the aged and the physically and mentally disabled.

Violence

Broadcasting service licensees must not broadcast material which, judged within context:

- contains violence which does not play an integral role in developing the plot, character or theme of the material as a whole, or sanctions, promotes or glamorises violence or unlawful conduct;

- sanctions, promotes or glamorises violence or unlawful conduct based on race, national or ethnic origin, colour, religion, gender, sexual orientation, age, or mental or physical disability; and

- amounts to propaganda for war, incitement of imminent violence, or the advocacy of hatred that is based on race, ethnicity, religion or gender and that constitutes incitement to cause harm;

- contains gratuitous violence in any form i.e. violence which does not play an integral role in developing the plot, character or theme of the material as a whole, sanctions, promotes or glamorizes violence.

These do not apply to a broadcast which:

- judged within context, amounts to a *bona fide* scientific, documentary, dramatic, artistic or religious broadcast;

- amounts to a discussion, argument or opinion on a matter pertaining to religion, belief or conscience; or

- amounts to a *bona fide* discussion, argument or opinion on a matter of public interest.

Violence against women

Broadcasters shall:

- not broadcast material which, judged within context, sanctions, promotes or glamorises any aspect of violence against women;

- ensure that women are not depicted as victims of violence unless the violence is integral to the story being told; and

- be particularly sensitive not to perpetuate the link between women in a sexual context and women as victims of violence.

- Children

Broadcasting service licensees must not broadcast material which is harmful or disturbing to children at times when a large number of children are likely to be part of the audience.

Broadcasting service licensees must exercise particular caution, as provided below, in the depiction of violence in children's programming.

In children's programming portrayed by real-life characters, violence may, whether physical, verbal or emotional, only be portrayed when it is essential to the development of a character and plot.

Animated programming for children, while accepted as a stylised form of story-telling which may contain non-realistic violence, must not have violence as its central theme, and must not incite dangerous imitation.

Programming for children must with reasonable care deal with themes that could threaten their sense of security when portraying, for example, domestic conflict, death, crime or the use of drugs or alcohol.

Programming for children must with reasonable care deal with themes which could influence children to imitate acts which they see on screen or hear about, such as the use of plastic bags as toys, the use of matches or the use of dangerous household object as toys.

Programming for children must not contain realistic scenes of violence which create the impression that violence is the preferred or only method to resolve conflict between individuals.

Programming for children must not contain realistic scenes of violence which minimise or gloss over the effect of violent acts. Any realistic depictions of violence must portray, in human terms, the consequences of that violence to its victims and its perpetrators.

Programming for children must not contain frightening or otherwise excessive special effects not required by the story line.

Offensive language, including profanity and other religiously insensitive material, must not be broadcast in programmes specially designed for children.

No excessively or grossly offensive language should be used before the watershed period on television or at times when a large number of children is likely to be part of the audience on television or radio.

Programming on television which contains scenes of explicit violence and/or sexual conduct and/or nudity and/or grossly offensive language intended for adult audiences must not be broadcast before the watershed period (between 21:00 and 05:00 for free-to-air television broadcasting service licensees and 20:00 and 05:00 for subscription television broadcasting service licensees).

Promotional material and music videos which contain scenes of explicit violence and/or explicit threatening violence and/or sexual conduct and/or the fondling or touching of breasts and/or genitalia or the anus and/or nudity and/or offensive language intended for adult audiences must not be broadcast before the watershed period.

Some programmes broadcast outside the watershed period may not be suitable for very young children. Licensees must provide sufficient information, in terms of regular scheduling patterns or audience advisories, to assist parents and *de facto* or legal guardians to make appropriate viewing choices.

Television broadcasting service licensees may, with the advance of the watershed period, progressively broadcast more adult material.

Broadcasting service licensees must be particularly sensitive to the likelihood that programmes which commence during the watershed period and which run beyond it may then be viewed by children.

Sexual Conduct

"Sexual conduct" means the display of genitals or of the anus, masturbation, sexual intercourse including anal sexual intercourse – in the case of child pornography, the fondling or touching of breasts, genitalia or the anus, the penetration of a vagina or anus with any object, oral genital contact, or oral anal contact.

Broadcasting service licensees must not broadcast material which, judged within context, contains a scene or scenes, simulated or real, of any of the following: child pornography, bestiality, sexual conduct which degrades a person in the sense that it advocates a particular form of hatred based on gender and which constitutes incitement to cause harm, explicit sexual conduct, explicit extreme violence or the explicit effects thereof, or explicit infliction of domestic violence.

These do not apply to *bona fide* scientific, documentary, dramatic or artistic material which, judged within context, is of such a nature; provided that it is broadcast with due audience advisory after the watershed on a sliding scale according to its content.

Scenes depiction sexual conduct, as defined in the Films and Publication Act 65 of 1996, should be broadcast only during the watershed period. Exceptions to this may be allowed in programmes with a serious educational purpose or where the representation is non-explicit and should be approved in advance by the most senior programme executive or a delegated alternate.

Explicit portrayal of violent sexual behaviour is justifiable only exceptionally and the same approval process as referred to above must be followed.

Offensive language including profanity, blasphemy and other religiously insensitive material shall not be used in programmes specially designed for children.

Paying a criminal for information

No payment shall be made to persons involved in crime or other notorious behaviour, or to persons who have been engaged in crime or other notorious behaviour, in order to obtain information concerning any such behaviour, unless compelling societal interests indicate the contrary.

Some procedural matters:

- When at any stage of the proceedings, the Chairperson is of the opinion that it is in the interest of fairness that a complainant must waive his or her rights to further legal recourse, the Chairperson shall require the complainant to waive such rights. If a complaint deals with a matter already before a South African Court the Commission will not consider it; and

- Under the Act, the Authority has the power to impose sanctions, including fines, on licensees who do not comply with this Code of Conduct.

THE OCTOBER 2012 WORKSHOPS

Journalists from Seychelles and UOM students and academics at the Gender Sensitive Reporting workshop

A session on gender in the media by Gender Links representatives

Participants analysing media content

Discussing ethics in television content

Pictures courtesy of Gender Links and Horatio Caine

www.ingramcontent.com/pod-product-compliance
Lightning Source LLC
Chambersburg PA
CBHW060038030426

42334CB00019B/2381